ISBN 9798869097538 (Paperback) | ISBN 9798869097545 (eBook)

Manufactured in the United States

Inexperienced

By

Karmen Scott

*Note to readers: this story contains "*ebonics*" and some profanity.

According to Google, *ebonics* "is African American English, especially when viewed as a language in its own right rather than as a dialect of standard English."

Table of Contents

Dedication

To young Karmen:

The girl who went to college with only ideas and inspiration for this series. You went off to school with no experience but was ready to face it all. You kept God in your heart as you openly observed people. You sat in your room many nights writing out all your ideas and now you get to share it with other people. Though you didn't meet your person your freshman year of college, you had yourself to love knowing that one day God would bless you to meet your special man. But perhaps your freshman year was less about finding someone and all about finding yourself. And I'd say you did a pretty good job. Now you are a published author which was only once a dream. I am so proud of you and encourage you to keep reaching for your dreams. You have accomplished so much already and now, you've accomplished this. Congratulations on the republishing of your very first novel. Who knows… Maybe you'll inspire a movie or TV show…

Chapter 1

"Rather, as servants of God we commend ourselves in every way: in great endurance; in troubles, hardships and distresses; in beatings, imprisonments and riots; in hard work, sleepless nights and hunger; in purity, understanding, patience and kindness; in the Holy Spirit and sincere love;" (2 Corinthians 6:4-6)

September 2014

Being a Christian can be very difficult. People often look at you funny when you tell them the things that you don't do and your beliefs. And I have temptations to do the wrong things sometimes. I know as a Christian, we're supposed to be an example, and I try to be that. But it can be hard. Like, sometimes I want to date the first guy that tells me I'm cute just because it's nice to know someone thinks I'm attractive. And if that's not hard enough, I at least want to kiss him. It can be very tough to not give in to peer pressure and do what all your friends are doing. It's about strength and where you are in your spiritual walk. I like to think I'm okay, but sometimes it can be tough. But Jesus never said following Him would be easy, as much as I wish it was.

“Kyrah! Kyrah!” my roommate yelled as she ran into my room. I looked at her like she had lost her mind.

“Is there a reason you’re calling my name like you’re being chased?”

She rolled her eyes, “Girl, bye.” I chuckled lightly and waited for her to finish talking. “Look, there’s a party tonight in Quentin’s room. You down?”

“I don’t know, Tamra. I have to study for a test next week, and-”

“Next week? Girl! You have a whole week. Plus, you’re always studying. Take a break, come on. There’s gonna be plenty of cuties there, and music, and drinks, and-”

I frowned, “Drinks? Oh, no. I will not be there. Thanks for the invite, though.” Tamra stared at me as if that was gonna make me change my mind. *A party does sound fun, and I could definitely use a break from studying. However, my breaks include PB&J sandwiches and Love & Hip Hop.*

“Well, if you change your mind, the party doesn’t end until whenever.”

I smiled, “Thanks. Have fun.” She gave a small smile and nodded. She left my room and I sighed in relief. As much as I wanted to go to that party, I didn’t feel right about it. I could just be paranoid, but I think I'll stick to my paranoia.

Hours went by and I was still studying. I get nervous about tests and I absolutely have to start studying in advance. I finally decide it's time for a break. I put my house shoes on, grabbed my room key, and walk out my door.

"Hey, where are you going?" Tamra asked me as I passed her room.

"Getting some candy. Be right back!" I proceeded to walk out my room and towards the elevator. I waited and waited as I toyed with my keys. The elevator doors finally opened. Once I got downstairs and into the vending room, I decided it would be best if I hurried up so I could get back to studying. As I was putting my change into the machine, another person walked in and waited for me to finish. I didn't know who it was, nor did I care. I just wanted to get out of there. People make me nervous. *Please don't speak to me. Please don't speak to me,* I thought to myself repeatedly.

"You don't look like you're going to a party", a deep voice said from behind me. I rolled my eyes and contemplated on if I wanted to respond or ignore the stranger. I decided to be nice and make eye contact with him. Only, I wish I wouldn't have done that. In that very moment, all I saw was absolute beauty. His chocolate eyes were captivating, along with his perfect smile, as his locs hung neatly to his shoulders. I stopped myself from staring and cleared my throat.

I looked him up and down, "I see I'm not the only one."

He chuckled making me melt a little inside. "I like to be fashionably late."

I smirked, "That makes one of us." I bent to get my candy and I felt his eyes on me. I smiled inwardly and looked back at him. He focused his eyes on my face and frowned.

"You're not going for real?"

I shook my head no. "Not a chance. I have some studying to get done. Plus, parties aren't really my scene."

He nodded and smiled, "I understand." I nodded in agreement. We stood there in silence for a while until he broke it, "Well, I hope you pass your test."

I smiled, "Thanks. Have fun at the party."

He shrugged as a smirk formed on his lips. "I'll try. Have a good night."

"You too." I walked out of the vending room and proceeded to the elevator. I got on the elevator and waited for it to land on my floor. Just as I was about to open my door, both of my roommates were walking out.

"Kyrah, are you sure you don't wanna come?" Tamra asked.

"Yeah, come on, Ky. Have some fun", my other roommate, Raynah said with a smile.

I shook my head, "I promise, I'm fine. Go have fun. I'll see you guys tomorrow." They nodded and walked down the hallway. I sighed and went into my room. I closed my suite door and lied on my bed. As I closed my eyes, all I could see was that boy's face. He was so perfect. He has that smile that could make anybody melt. And those eyes; they may not have been very significant to anybody else, but they were everything to me. And his hair. Lord knows I'm a sucker for locs. I prayed every night that God would bless me with a husband that had locs.

I spent a few moments thinking about "No Name", then I decided to resume studying while eating my Snicker's bar. I couldn't focus on studying, though. I was now contemplating on whether or not I wanted to go to the party. I wouldn't be going for the scenery, however, but to see *him*. I would go hoping that I would see him there, waiting to ask me for a dance. But that's only a fantasy. Besides, he's more than likely there dancing with some other girl. Just because he talked to me doesn't mean he was into me. Maybe he was just being nice.

After hours of trying to study, I finally gave up and called it a night. I had a whole week, after all. I changed into my PJ's, turned my light off, said my prayers and dozed off into a deep sleep.

Chapter 2

"But I tell you that anyone who looks at a woman lustfully has already committed adultery with her in his heart." (Matthew 5:28)

"Okay, that's all the notes I have for you guys today, so, we're super early. But I hope you all have a good weekend. See ya later, guys", my English professor said.

I packed my things and hurried out of the classroom. I was so hungry that I think I passed out at least three times while being in that class. It was the only class I had today, so I figured I could stop by one of the restaurants on campus and buy something. Thank God there weren't a lot of people in line, so I was able to get in and get out. As I was walking out, I accidently bumped into someone… Or they bumped into me, causing my books and food to fall out of my hands and spill all over the ground. *I knew I should have checked to see if my food was completely closed.*

"Yo, my bad! I didn't see you there", the familiar voice said. I hadn't even looked at the person because I was too busy cursing him out in my head while looking at my ruined food.

I sighed, “It’s fine. I should’ve watched where I was going.” We both bent down to pick of my books and some of the food that had fallen out. Once I finally looked up, I stopped what I was doing. *Him.*

“Nah, this was definitely my fault. Let me…”, he drifted off as he looked at me, finally realizing who I was. We stared at each other for a while, until he cleared his throat.

“Um… Let me pay for your meal.”

I shook my head, “I couldn’t ask you to do that. Really, it’s not—”

“You didn’t, I’m offering”, he replied slyly with a smirk. *Oh, dear Jesus. Help me not to lust after this man.* We both stood up slowly as he handed me my books. He had his hair pulled back today, showing of his perfect face. Was it possible to want to kiss someone you don’t know? That’s exactly what I wanted to do. I wanted him… Badly.

I shrugged, trying to play it cool, “If you insist.” He smiled and motioned for me to walk ahead of him. We walked silently back into the restaurant and I ordered my food.

“Okay, that’ll be $7.92”, the cashier said looking at me.

"I got it", No Name said. He paid the cashier and he handed me my food. We walked back outside and stood there.

"Thanks, for paying for my food", I said looking down.

"No problem. I kinda owed you", he said with a chuckle. "So, what's your name? I didn't get it the other night."

"Kyrah. What's yours?"

"Anthony."

I smiled and nodded, finally looking him in the eyes. He is just the most perfect thing I've ever seen. And every day I see plenty of cute boys, but none of them came close to him. I don't even know him, but I do know he is perfect. Did I mention he was perfect?

"Nice to formally meet you."

"You too", he smiled.

We began walking back to our building, and surprisingly, we kept talking the whole time. I was actually surprised at how well we could hold a conversation. The walk back to our building ended too quickly. We stopped right in front of the entrance door.

"I hope this isn't too forward, but I was wondering if I could have your number", he said.

I was so surprised; I couldn't really think of the word I was looking for. *Yes, Kyrah. Say yes.* "Uh- yes! I mean, yeah, sure. I don't see why not."

He smiled, "A'ight, bet." I blushed taking his phone as he handed it to me. I put my number in and handed it back to him.

"Well, I'll let you go. I'll see you around and I'll text you later."

I smiled and nodded, "I'll be looking forward to it." *Wow. Did I really just say that? I hope I don't sound too desperate.* He smiled and began to back up still looking at me. I proceeded to walk in the building, and quickly hurried to my floor. I walked in my room and saw my roommates watching TV in the living room area.

"Girl, you got food without us?" Tamra asked.

I frowned, "What?" I looked down at the bag of food I was holding. *How did I forget about that? I'm not even hungry anymore.* "Oh, yeah. Sorry. I almost died from hunger in class today."

They laughed. "It's cool. We ate. Sit. We're watching Love and Hip Hop", Raynah said. I nodded, setting my books, purse, and food on the table. I looked at the food with a funny feeling in my stomach. Not sure if it was the fact that I was still hungry or butterflies from Anthony, I began to eat my food silently.

"Hey, what's up with you? You've been quiet since you walked in earlier", Tamra asked. It was just Tamra and me sitting in the living room doing schoolwork since Raynah was hanging out with her boyfriend.

I shrugged, "I'm always quiet."

"True, but you're extra quiet", she emphasized while shaking her head. "What's going on?"

I looked at her so she wouldn't suspect anything. I wasn't ready to tell them about Anthony. It was way too early to even know if he and I would go past being acquaintances. I want us to get to know each other, but I didn't want to tell them I met someone because they would just blow it up into this big thing that wasn't even serious.

"I'm fine, Tam. I'm just a little tired. And I was super hungry earlier", I replied still looking at her. She side-eyed me for a second, then finally nodded. I silently exhaled, thankful that she let it go… This time. I focused in back on my homework when suddenly my phone started going off. I frowned, looking at the unknown number. *Who is this? Oh… Anthony.*

Hey, this is Ant. Is this Kyrah?

I smiled to myself as I texted him back:

Hey, yes, it is. (:

I looked up and found Tamra staring at me.

"What?" I said pretending to be clueless, although I already knew why she was staring at me.

"You. Met. Somebody." she said as a smile slowly began to form on her face. My cover was completely blown now. I couldn't even last a whole day without at least one of my roommates prying in my business. Normally I was hard to read, but I guess talking to Anthony made me an open book. And I wasn't sure if that was a good thing or a bad thing.

"What are you talking about?" I asked trying to play it off, although I know she knew that I knew what she was talking about… If that makes any sense.

"You met a guy. I peeped you look down at your phone and smile all big. That's why you're so quiet. You're thinking about him. You like him!" She turned her entire body towards me, with a big smile on her face. "Who is it?"

"Tam, it's nobody. I was laughing at something my best friend said. I didn't meet anybody", I lied completely out of the side of my neck. *Hopefully she'll buy it.*

"Kyrah-"

"It's nobody! Leave me alone."

She side-eyed me once again, “Mmhm, I’m gonna figure out who it is. That wasn’t a laughing smirk, that was a ‘I got a boo and he said something sexy’ smirk. I’m gon’ figure it out whether you want me to or not.”

I rolled my eyes, sighing. “Do you, Tamra.”

“I intend to”, she replied with a cocky smile.

It’s 9:00 p.m. and I’m the only one in my whole suite. Both my roomies are off with some friends and I’m in my room studying once again… Well, sort of.

“I’m coming to your room to keep you company.”

I chuckled, “That won’t be necessary, Anthony. I’m okay.” We had been on the phone for about an hour just talking and getting to know each other. I found out that he’s two years older than I am, and he found out that I’m a nerd.

“I ain’t ask you that. I’m coming. What’s your room number?”

I breathed silently. *Why was that so attractive? I need to put an end to this conversation.* “I’m not telling you my room number. We just met. I don’t know if you’re crazy or not.”

He laughed, “What? Be for real. Why won’t you let me come up there?”

I cleared my throat, “I don’t think it would be appropriate right now.” It was silent for a few seconds. I began to regret saying that, or even saying “no”. Why couldn’t I just let him come keep me company? What’s the harm in that?

“Oh… You’re afraid of what you might do?” *Yes.*

I inhaled sharply, trying to think of what to say. *Get off the phone.* “I gotta… uh, go. I need to finish some homework and get some studying done.”

He chuckled, “I didn’t mean to make you uncomfortable. You don’t have to get off the phone. I’m off that. We can talk about something else.”

I sighed, “Promise?”

He chuckled again, “Promise.”

I smiled. We talked on the phone for another hour until we both decided to get ready for bed. I went to bed with the biggest smile on my face. I mean, how often does a girl get to talk to a guy that she was instantly attracted to at first glance? I didn’t think we’d get past our small chat at the vending machine, but I’ve never been more thankful to run into a stranger more than once.

I said my prayers and stared at the ceiling. I prayed that God reveal to me that this is what He wants. I like Anthony so far, at least I think I do. But I don’t even know if he’s saved or not. And I find myself wanting him in a way that’s not normal for me. Honestly, that’s why I didn’t want him to come up here. I know how college boys can be and honestly, with me liking him, that would make saying “no” much harder. I thank God for giving me the guts to actually say “no” to him even coming up here to “keep me company”. I would like to think that it’s a part of God’s will for me to be with Anthony, but after our phone conversation, I’m not so sure…

He laughed, “Better watch your back.” I laughed along with him.

“Well, I’ma let you go. I’ll call you later.”

“Okay”, I said with a pouty face. He chuckled and hugged me. He kissed my forehead making me blush. We parted, said our final goodbyes, and I walked in my suite. I watched him walk away until he disappeared around the corner. I closed the door only to find Tamra standing right there. I screamed, holding my chest.

“TAMRA! WHAT THE HELL IS WRONG WITH YOU!?” I yelled.

She laughed, “Sorry! But don’t try and flip this on me! Did you just cuss?? Who was that guy??”

I frowned, “What guy?” Although I knew she knew I was playing dumb, it was fun to mess with her.

“Kyrah, I swear if you don’t stop playing with me-”

“OK! Okay… Jeez. Let me get comfy and I’ll tell you and Raynah all about it. Give me a minute.”

She squealed, with a huge smile on her face, “Okay!” She ran off into Raynah’s room as I made my way to my room. I sighed. *I really hope they don’t make a huge deal out of this.*

After about ten minutes of getting in my comfortable attire, I grabbed my phone and made my way to the living room area. I spotted Tamra and Raynah waiting for me on the couch with a big bowl of popcorn and three cans of soda on the table.

“About time! Hurry and sit!” Tamra exclaimed patting the spot between her and Raynah.

“You have so much explaining to do”, Raynah said.

“I concur”, Tamra added.

I sighed and carefully sat in between them. I don’t know why I’m so nervous to tell them about Anthony. I’ve never been so serious about anyone. I’ve liked guys, yeah, but it’s never gone further than that. If Anthony were to become my boyfriend, he would be my first. And I guess because I’m so new to this whole dating thing, I don’t really know how to explain what’s going on between us.

“Okay… Where do I start?” I asked more to myself, but of course, Tamra had a smart rebuttal.

“How about the beginning? That always works”, she replied.

I rolled my eyes, “Fine. Okay, so when I went to get candy the night of that party you guys went to a few weeks ago, he came out of nowhere and started talking to me about if I was going to the party. I said no and he said good luck on your test. Follow me?" They nodded, looking at me intensely.

"Wait, so you didn't get his name?" Raynah asked.

"Not at this point." She nodded.

I told them everything and they listened eagerly, asking me questions. However, I purposefully excluded our little phone conversation because I didn't want them to make a big deal about it. Although they're always in my business, they have my back. I can't even imagine how they'd react to know that he made a sexual suggestion towards me. I just chose to put that out of my mind and forget it ever happened. I like Anthony and I want this to go somewhere.

"Aw, this is cute. Our little Kyrah is going on a date", Raynah cooed while pinching my cheeks.

I laughed, "I really like him, guys. He's so… I don't know. He's just different. He comes off pretty strong and he's pretty forward, but he's respectable with it. He's such a gentleman."

Tamra smiled and nodded. "I can tell. He seems to be in a good head space. He walked you to your room. I haven't met a single guy that's wanted to talk to me and is willing to do something like that... Does he have a brother?"

Rayna and I laughed. “You’re a mess. He does and he’s married.” She rolled her eyes and grunted in disappointment. Suddenly there was a knock on the door that interrupted our laughing session. Everyone just sat there until they both looked at me.

“Really? Wow.” I slowly got out of my comfortable spot and walked to the door. As I looked through the peephole, I saw Anthony. My heartbeat accelerated and I blushed. I slowly opened the door and he stood there looking at me with a smile on his face.

“Miss me already?” I joked.

“Of course,” He chuckled, “I actually came to get my math book. I think you grabbed it by accident.”

“Oh, I’m so sorry! Come with me and I’ll give it to you.” He nodded and followed me into the suite.

“Hello, ladies”, he greeted Tamra and Raynah.

The greeted him back as he followed me to room. I searched through my bag and pulled out his math book.

“Here you go. Sorry about that”, I said handing it to him.

He smiled as he took it, and also grabbed one of my hands. He looked me in my eyes, “Don’t sweat it.” I smiled staring him back in the eyes. We stayed like that for a moment. It was nice. It was… luring, innocent. *I could stare in his eyes all day. He is just so beautiful.*

"Well, I'm gonna go. I'll call you later. I can't wait until Friday", he said still holding my hand.

"Neither can I", I said as another smile crept its way onto my face. "But I'll be waiting for that phone call."

He chuckled, "I bet. Try not to miss me so much." I laughed and rolled my eyes. We walked out of my room still holding hands until we reached the main door.

"See you later", he said as he turned towards me. He kissed me on the cheek. I hesitated to let go of his roughly soft hand. He smirked while opening the door. "You ladies have a good night", he said to Tam and Raynah.

"You too", they said almost in unison. He winked at me and made his way out the door. I closed the door and let out a long breath. It felt like I had been holding my breath the whole time he was there.

"Girl! He is fine!" Tamra said pretty loudly.

I giggled, "I know right!?" We all laughed as I ran back to the couch and plopped in between them.

"You guys look so good together. I can tell he really likes you. He couldn't care less about that damn math book. He just wanted to see you again. And the way he looks at you... So romantic", Tamra gushed.

"I know right? I wish Tommy would look at me like that", Raynah said. Tamra rolled her eyes, "We ain't talking about him right now." We all laughed.

Well, that went better than I expected... I hope everything goes smoothly from here.

Chapter 4

"Whoever sows to please their flesh, from the flesh will reap destruction; whoever sows to please the Spirit, from the Spirit will reap eternal life." (Galatians 6:8)

It's Friday. 5:00 p.m. And what am I doing? Watching YouTube videos. I was starting to rethink this whole date. I was so nervous, although I wanted to go. Something was holding me. It was mainly because I've never been on one before with anybody and I'm new to these kinds of feelings. I feel something different with Anthony. It's slightly deeper than just a crush and I guess I'm a little afraid to go further.

After procrastinating, I finally decided to start getting ready. A few times, I was tempted to text Anthony and tell him some kind of lie to get me out of it, but I decided against it. If I didn't go on a date now, I never would. I took another shower, picked out my outfit, then started on my hair and makeup. Since this would be my first date ever, I decided to keep it simple. I settled on a ripped pair of black skinny jeans, a white t-shirt, a denim jacket, and my black wedge heel sandals. I kept my makeup as simple as I could and put my hair up in my signature afro puff. I put my class ring from high school on, big silver hoop earrings, and a few bracelets on. After spraying myself with some perfume, I checked myself in the mirror.

"Girl, you look hot!" Tamra said as she walked in my room.

I looked at my body then back at her nervously, "Really? It's not too much?"

"No, it's perfect. What's the matter?" she frowned with concern.

I sighed and shrugged. "I don't know. I'm just so nervous. This is my first date. Ever. I'm feeling things for Anthony that I've never felt for anybody else. I know it's not love, yet. It's way too soon, but... It's developing to that and I'm so afraid of the thought of that because we just met. I'm so scared of losing myself in a guy. I'm a virgin and I don't want him to take advantage of me, but I'm not as worried about him as I am myself. I'm just afraid of liking... Loving him so much that I compromise myself. I've always been so content and comfortable with being alone. I like it that way. This... is different for me. This night could change everything."

After I finished talking, I felt some sort of relief. It was almost as if I'd been wanting to say that for a while. I looked at Tamra who was smiling. I frowned in confusion.

"Why are you smiling? I just poured my heart out to you."

She chuckled, "I'm smiling because that's the first time you've ever really opened up to me. Look, I know we haven't known each other long, but I do know one thing for sure, you have a good head on your shoulders. Listen, you have to just go with the flow. You like him, so what? There's no harm in that. Now is your time to learn how to fall in love and really open up to someone. I can tell he really likes you. Go on this date and have fun. Enjoy him, enjoy yourself. Relax. You guys aren't getting married. It's just a date."

I smiled, "You're right. I think I'm okay now. I'm still nervous, though. Thanks, TamTam." She smiled and gave me a hug. After we parted, there was a knock on the door. I checked the clock to see what time it was. *7:00.*

"I'll get it!" Raynah yelled as she went to answer the door. I grabbed my room key, phone, and my purse, turned off my room light and closed the door. I heard Anthony's voice from afar and my heart began to beat faster. I took a deep breath before making my way into the common area. Once I approached where everyone was, Anthony looked at me. A smile crept up on his face as he looked me up and down in admiration.

"Hi", I said moving closer.

“Hi. You look… Beautiful”, he said looking me in the eyes.

I blushed as a smile formed on my lips, “Thank you. You look very handsome.”

He chuckled and stroked his neat beard, “Well… Ya’ know.”

I laughed, “Shut up.”

Raynah and Tamra just stood there looking at us until Tamra cleared her throat. “You two love birds should get going. You have all night to stare at each other and undress each other with your eyes.”

“Really??!” I exclaimed as I frowned.

“It was a joke! Now leave! Have fun!”

Anthony held out his hand for me to grab and we left the room hand-in-hand. *Here we go…*

“You look really beautiful. Not that you don’t always… But you got all cute for me”, Anthony said with a smile. We were at Chili’s for dinner before our movie.

I smirked, “Don’t be feeling yourself over there. I got cute because I wanted to.”

He laughed, "Oh, it's like that?" I giggled and nodded. We talked for a little while before our waiter came to take our drink orders.

"Ok, I'll be right back with your drinks. Would you guys like an appetizer?"

Anthony nodded before ordering our appetizer. The waiter walked away leaving us alone.

"Be honest", he began. I nodded in agreement. "What do you want from me? I really like you. I want us to go somewhere. I just need you to tell me what you need from me."

I took a deep breath, "I mean … I don't know. This is all new for me."

He stared into my eyes, "What is?"

I sighed, "Don't laugh. I've never been on a date before. I've never even had a boyfriend. All of this—these feelings are new for me. I'm very hesitant about being with anybody because I've been so comfortable being by myself. So, honestly, I don't know what I want."

He reached across the table for my hand, so I placed mine in his. He caressed my hand with his thumb. "But you do know. You just told me without really sayin' it. You're the independent type. You're stubborn, too. And a smartass." We laughed as he continued, "But you need someone that will spoil you anyway. And someone who will be there and show you that instead of just saying that. I wanna be your support system, your shoulder, your happiness, your annoyance, all'at and more. Give me a chance. Allow this date to be the beginning of something beautiful. But you can't run from me, a'ight?"

I sighed in happiness as I smiled. I held back the happy tears that threatened to come out. "I won't run." He smiled and he kissed the back of my hand. Just then our waiter came back with our drinks. We ordered our food and ate soon after. After we finished our dinner and Anthony paid, we walked across the street to the movie theatre for the rest of our date.

We were back at our dorm and Anthony was walking me to my room.

"I had a really great time tonight. Thanks for taking me out. I didn't know guys still did that", I said while smiling at him.

He chuckled, "Well, you got lucky."

I playfully hit him in the arm while laughing, "Shut up. You're so annoying."

He moved closer to me, closing the gap between us while holding my hands. "But you like me anyway."

His eyes moved from my eyes to my lips. My breath hitched as he inched closer and closer.

“You’re right. I do”, I finally replied.

We just looked at each other, both our eyes repeatedly looking at each other’s lips.

“I wanna kiss you, if that’s okay.”

I nodded my head, “Definitely okay.” He smirked as he leaned in closer. I closed my eyes and leaned in to meet him. My heartbeat picked up a bajillion times faster than normal. He teased me by making our lips touch, but not enough for a full kiss.

“Kiss me already”, I whispered as my breath became shorter. He smiled as he kissed me. *Finally. This is the best feeling in the world.* We kissed for what felt like eternity. He was gentle, yet eager. He removed his hands from mine, placing them on my lower back. I wrapped my arms around his neck as we moved closer to one another. We kissed and kissed, not wanting to let go. It was absolutely magical, and I didn’t want it to end.

We finally parted, both exhaling deeply. We laughed lightly, still holding each other.

“Your lips are as soft as I imagined”, he said. I blushed and looked at our feet. “I should get going”, he said.

I nodded, getting sad. "Okay. Well, text me when you get to your room, so I'll know you made it."

He laughed, "I'm just going downstairs."

I rolled my eyes, "Things happen. Just do it. I just wanna make sure you're safe."

He smiled, "Okay. I will."

I held out my pinky, "Promise?"

He wrapped his pinky around mine and kissed me one last time, "I promise." I smiled as we parted completely. "See you tomorrow", he said as I opened my door.

"Tomorrow", I replied with a wink. I walked in my room to Tamra and Raynah sitting on the couch watching TV. I turned around to wave at Anthony one last time. He waved back and walked away. I closed the door and turned around to look at my roommates with a huge smile on face.

"I take it your date went well?" Tamra said sitting up with a smile.

I nodded and gushed, "Guys, he's so romantic. He's perfect."

They squealed while running towards me to pull towards the couch.

"Tell us everything!" Raynah exclaimed.

I sit down on the couch between them and tell them every single detail of the date. Butterflies flew around in my stomach just at the mention of Anthony's name. They both stared at me intently with smiles on their faces as I told them how he was such a gentleman and how he admitted how much he really likes me.

"But the best part… That kiss," I finished as I leaned back on the couch and closed my eyes.

"You guys kissed??!" Tamra asked excitedly.

I nodded eagerly. "He was so gentle. It was so perfect. Everything was perfect."

"Aw, that's so sweet! I'm glad you guys had a good time. He's such a nice guy. He looked at you like you were the only person on earth when you walked in here", Tamra said.

I blushed before my phone vibrated. I checked my phone and smiled when I saw it was from Anthony.

I made it to my room. Lol

What a wonderful night…

Chapter 5

"To this you were called, because Christ suffered for you, leaving you an example, that you should follow in his steps." (1 Peter 2:21)

It's been one month since Anthony and I started dating and everything was going great. I've managed to stay focused on my schoolwork while still giving him some of my time. I even still make time for God. Since we've been dating for a while, I wanted to talk to him about his relationship with God. I was nervous about bringing it up, but it has to be done.

He and I were sitting at in the common area of my room. I decide it would be best to just wait to ask him about his salvation later. I didn't want to ruin the mood.

"Where are you taking me tonight?" I asked while we lounged on the couch with my feet in his lap.

He chuckled, "Why? That's none of your business."

I pouted and folded my arms. "I need to know what to wear."

"Doesn't matter what you wear. You'll be sexy either way." He smiled slyly to himself avoiding eye contact with me. I gave him a blank stare waiting for him to look at me.

“I know you see me looking at you”, I finally said.

He nodded, “I do. That don’t mean I gotta look at you.”

I rolled my eyes, “Whatever. I’m gonna show up in sweats and a tank top.”

He looked at me and smiled, “And you’ll still be beautiful. Do you, babygirl.”

I giggled as I leaned in to kiss him on the cheek. “Do you still want me to retwist your hair, baby?” He nodded. He got off the couch and sat on the floor while I left to get some gel and a comb. As soon as I sat down, I started on his hair while we watched TV.

About an hour and half later, I was done with his hair, and we decided to hang out for little bit before we both had to get ready for our date. It was now 6:30 and Anthony and I were standing at the door so he could leave to get ready.

“I’ll be back in an hour, okay?” he said looking at me with love in his eyes. Just the exchange set the butterflies in my stomach off.

“Okay, I’ll be ready.” He smiled before leaning down to kiss me sweetly. We parted after a few seconds then he left.

"Time to go get ready", I said to myself.

~~~

Anthony and I pulled up to a nice art gallery and my mouth dropped. I looked at him and smiled.

"Oh, this is so nice! Come on!" I exclaimed unbuckling my seatbelt.

He laughed, "Wait, baby! Don't be in such a hurry. You know better than to open that door, too."

I laughed and rolled my eyes, "Okay, okay. Fine." I impatiently waited for him to come open the passenger door so we could go inside. Anthony knew how much I wanted to go to the art gallery. It was nice to know that he was paying attention to me.

After waiting for what felt like a century, he finally opened my door and we walked in the gallery hand-in-hand. We took a tour, but eventually ventured off to do our own thing. The tour guide was talking too much for us, so we did our tour alone. We spent about an hour and a half at the gallery until both of us got hungry. He then took me to a nice café with live local entertainment.

I ate in silence debating on how to bring up a relationship with God. I knew it had to be done, but I wasn't sure know how to. I really like and care about Anthony more than I have anybody, and I don't want
~~~

to lose him over something so simple, yet important. I played with my food as we listened to the person singing on stage. I avoided eye contact with Anthony so he wouldn't know something was up, although I don't think it worked.

"What's on your mind, babygirl?" he asked as he looked at me sincerely. *Nope. Didn't work.*

I shrugged, giving him a fake smile, "Nothing. Why would something be up?"

He smirked, "Because your whole demeanor has changed, completely. You're playing with your food, and you won't look at me."

I sighed, finally giving in. I looked at him with caution, "I need to talk to you. It's important. It's nothing bad… It's just really important to me."

"Go ahead, babe." *Here we go…*

"I was just wondering… Well, you know I'm a Christian and it's important for me to know where you are in your faith. I didn't wanna ask because I didn't wanna come off too pushy, and you don't have to answer right now if you don't want to, but I'm just putting it out there. And I'll stop talking now…"

He chuckled, "You are so cute."

I blushed, "Thanks."

He nodded. "Well, to answer your question, I guess I'm not. I've never really taken it seriously. It's just something I've never thought about. I went to church when I was younger, but my parents never really taught me what it really meant to be one, so I didn't ask. I didn't care. I suppose it's not that big a deal in my life. I know it should be, but… I don't know."

I listened to him attentively. Everything he was saying was breaking my heart. Not because of him, but because he had no idea how important it is. He had no idea how much God wants a relationship with him.

"Well… Would you be interested in knowing more about it? I could show you", I suggested.

He smiled, "I would actually like that very much." I smiled inwardly and outwardly.

~~~

"I talked to him about his faith at dinner tonight", I told my mom. It was about 10:00 p.m. and my mom called me to say goodnight.

"Really? What did he say?"

I shrugged as if she could see me, "He told me that he wasn't a Christian and that it had never really been important to him because his parents never really taught it to him. He knows he should take it more seriously, but he just never knew much about it. I
~~~

offered to teach him more about it and he was happy to learn. So hopefully I can be the best example to bring him to accept Christ."

"Well, that's good. At least he's open to it. That's the first step. At least he didn't just turn you away and brush it off. But make sure he doesn't just get saved because of you."

"Yeah, I will. I know he really likes me, and I don't want that to be the only reason he's interested in learning about God. But he seemed very genuine."

"Good, good. Well, I'll be in prayer. I'll let you go. Goodnight. Love you."

"Goodnight. Love you too." I pressed "End" and sat my phone down on my dresser.

I wasn't too concerned about Anthony wanting to know more about God. If anything, I was super excited. I just pray that God will use me in the way He wants to. It would be so beautiful to know that I was used to help bring my boyfriend close to God. But I just wasn't sure what to do. Just be myself? I guess. But will he really pay attention, is the question…

Chapter 6

"Submit yourselves, then to God. Resist the devil, and he will flee from you." (James 4:7)

"Okay, class. Remember your papers are due Friday online. Do not forget. It's a five-point penalty every day it's late. That's not much, but it'll definitely add up. Please, turn them in on time. I'll see you guys next week", my professor announced while everyone packed their belongings. I was moving kind of slow, but eventually made my way out of the classroom. I needed a nap and I didn't feel like being bothered by anybody.

As I was slowly but surely walking back to my room, my phone vibrated in my hand.

Turn around.

It was a text from Anthony. I turned around and spotted him walking towards me.

"Hey", he greeted as he got closer with a big grin.

I gave him a tired smile and a wave.

He frowned, "What's wrong, mama?"

I shrugged, "I'm really tired. I need a nap."

He smirked. Somehow, I knew he was about to say something inappropriate. He's been extra touchy-feely and sexually passive this past week. I know we've been dating for a little over a month, but why is sex expected?

"Whatever it is you're thinking, keep it to yourself", I said holding my hand up.

"Damn. Okay", he said laughing. I didn't find it amusing. At all. But I gave a small smile.

"I'm gonna head to my room. Go to class. Call me later", I said grabbing one of his hands.

He chuckled, "Yes ma'am. I'll talk to you to a little later." He bent down and kissed me. My heart skipped a beat. No matter how many times we kiss, it had the same effect on me. I bit my lip once we parted and gave him a small smile. He winked.

We both went our separate ways and I got back to my room much faster than I thought I would.

"Tamra??? Raynah??? Somebody??" I called as I placed my bag and phone on the dining table. Raynah soon opened her door and walked out with a frown.

"You okay? Something wrong?" she asked concerned as she moved closer into the main area.

I shrugged, "I was just seeing if someone was here. But I need to talk. It's about Anthony."

She nodded, “A’ight. Let’s go in my room. Tamra’s in the room with some guy. I’m sure their doing stuff.”

I laughed, shaking my head, “Oh, gosh.” I followed her into her room, and she left the door cracked, but closed it enough where no one can just walk in.

“Okay, what’s up?” she asked as she sat on bed, patting a spot beside her.

I sighed, “Well… Anthony… He’s been extra touchy lately and his sexual comments are becoming extra frequent.”

“Like what?” she asked becoming curious.

“Okay, like yesterday while we were watching TV, he kept rubbing my butt and kissing me on my neck. I kept pushing him away, but I think he thought I was playing. Then he’s just been making comments that are basically hints saying that he wants some and when am I gonna give it to him.”

I stared at Raynah who was staring back at me.

“Raynah?”

“Well… Are you?”

“Am I what?” I asked slightly thrown off.

“Are you gonna give him some, girl?” she asked laughing a little.

I looked down at my hands in my lap and shook my head "no" feeling slightly embarrassed. There aren't very many eighteen-year-old virgins left in the world and I just happened to be one of them… By choice.

"Why not?" she asked out of curiosity.

"Well, for starters, I'm a virgin. And I also planned on waiting until I'm married."

"You're a virgin???" she asked shocked and a little loud.

I chuckled, "Yeah. Isn't it obvious?"

She shrugged, "I suppose so... But since you are…does he know?" Once again, I shook my head "no".

"It hasn't come up", I finally said.

"Well, bring it up. Let him know up front. Then you'll really know what kind of guy he is. If he's okay with it, then he'll stick around. If not, let him go. He can't make you do anything you don't want to do."

I sat and thought about that. She was right. I needed to be upfront with Anthony and let him know how I feel. I don't want to lead him on thinking I'm okay with it because I'm the complete opposite. Plus, this will just make it easier to say no. I realized I needed to do this ASAP because the longer I wait, the more prone I'll be to actually sleep with him when the time presents itself.

I looked at Raynah and smiled, "I'm gonna talk to him tonight."

She smiled, "Good." I gave her a hug and left her room. I grabbed my phone from the dining table and searched for Anthony's name.

Hey, let's go somewhere when you get out of class.

I impatiently waited for him to respond as I paced back and forth. My phone then vibrated slightly catching me off guard.

I'm game. Where you wanna go?

I thought about it for a second.

Starbucks sound ok?

Once again, I waited for him to text me back. He was in class so I knew there would be a slight delay in his response. After about five minutes, he finally responded:

Whatever you want, beautiful. I'll come get you when I get out of class, a'ight?

I smiled, blushing faintly.

Ok. See you then.

I checked the time and saw that I had about an hour and fifteen minutes to spare so I decided to take the nap that I had been anticipating all day.

“What made you want to hang out?” Anthony asked as we sat at a secluded table in Starbucks.

I smirked, “I can’t hang out with my boyfriend?”

He laughed, “Nah.” I gave him a straight face, which made him laugh harder.

“Shut up. You ain’t cute.” I rolled my eyes playful before taking a sip from my Caramel Frappuccino.

“Whatever. You wit’ me so that says a lot about you”, he joked before biting into his chocolate chip cookie. I laughed.

“I hate you, man”, I said finally calming down.

“Now, I know that’s a lie. You love me”, he said seriously.

I stuck my tongue out at him before sipping my coffee. He raised one of his eyebrows and smirked. Instantly, I became uncomfortable with what was probably about to come out of his mouth.

“Man… Why you be teasing me like that?” he said looking at me. I could see a difference in his eyes. I became annoyed with the fact that just sticking my tongue out at him turned him on. *This boy’s hormones are out of control.*

I shrugged, “I didn’t do anything. Why you always gotta go there?”

He chuckled, “Chill, babe.”

“No, I wanna know. Why do you always have to go there?”

He frowned in a way I’d never seen him frown before. “What you mean?”

“This past week, you have been real extra with the “gestures”. Why is your mind so far in the gutter these days?”

He sighed and just stared at me. He shook his head lightly, “Why you buggin’?”

I chuckled, “I’m buggin’? You’re not gonna answer my question?”

“Not if I don’t want to. I don’t have to answer to you.”

I nodded, “You’re right. You don’t. Cool.”

He looked at me, waiting for me to return it. Instead, I just kept drinking my coffee and played with my phone.

“Babe.” Ignore. “Babygirl.” Eyeroll. “Kyrah.” Ignore again.

“A’ight. Since you wanna act like that...” I shrugged and continued doing what I was doing. I wasn’t going to let him off so easily. *I don’t care how many pet names he calls me. He needs to know how his comments make me feel.*

“Look, we’re not leaving until we talk. So go ahead and get rid of all that attitude and talk to me. Put your phone down, please”, he said calmly while looking in my eye. *Oh, sweet Jesus…*

I rolled my eyes, trying to ignore my own hormones at this point. I placed my phone on the table, finally looking at him.

“Why you buggin’, boo?” he asked sincerely.

I sighed, “I’m bugging because you just kinda brushed the way I feel to the side. Your little sexual remarks and gestures make me uncomfortable. Like, is that all you expect out of me? Because I’m telling you right here, right now, you can forget it. I’m not into all that.”

He sat up straight in his seat, still looking me in the eyes. He sighed, “Sweetheart”, he grabbed my hands, “I’m not trying to make you uncomfortable. I appreciate you telling me how you feel. I don’t wanna make you feel like you have to do something you don’t wanna do. I’m sorry if I made you feel that way.”

I nodded. “And I’m sorry for getting all amped. I should’ve just talked to you”, I apologized. He smiled and kissed my hands.

"I'm not gon' lie, though. I do want you. It's gon' be hard to restrain myself", he admitted as he let go of my hands.

I couldn't lie either. I wanted him back. But I couldn't risk giving myself to him without knowing if we would still be together afterwards. It was too risky. I adore him, and I want to make him happy. However, if that's all he wants to make him happy, it wasn't going to happen. I couldn't do that. Not to myself, not to him, not to my future husband, and most importantly, to God. It's hard to say no to Anthony because I want to please him, but not just physically. I want our connection and our love to be deeper than that.

"Well, the feeling is mutual… Believe me. However, I'm not down with all that."

He nodded, "I get it. I get it. But are you…?"

I nodded already knowing what he was insinuating. "I am… a virgin, yes." He smirked. I frowned etched across my forehead.

"What?"

"Nothing. I'm just honored to be with you. Like, I've never been with anyone like you. You're so different. A good different. It's rare to find virgins these days. Sometimes I wish I would've waited because then arguments like the one we just had wouldn't have happened."

I sat there in shock that he had just admitted all of that to me. I couldn't quite find the words to say so I just nodded until something came to me.

"Well… You can always start over. Every minute is a new chance to get it right."

He shrugged, "Yeah, I guess. I don't feel like I can, though. Like, it's too late. That's why I'm not a Christian. I feel like I'm not… Good enough, I guess."

"That's not true, though. All you have to do is accept Jesus's perfect sacrifice. It's never too late. It's only too late when you're no longer breathing. Every breath you take is a chance to make a change."

He nodded, "Yeah…" I could sense him distancing himself mentally from this conversation, so I decided to leave it alone. I thought carefully before responding.

"Well, I'm not gonna push you into anything, but if you wanna talk about it anytime, I'm here."

"I know, baby."

I smiled, nodding.

We left Starbucks about ten minutes later. The car ride was silent, but it was a comfortable silence. It was actually comfortable enough for me to fall asleep. We held hands the whole ride and by the time we reached the school, I was knocked out.

"Babygirl, we here", Anthony said tapping me on the leg. I frowned hoping it was a dream. I was sleeping too well to even move. He laughed, "Baby, come on before I put you on Snapchat."

I grunted and finally opened my eyes. I looked at him and gave him a warning eye.

"You better not put me on there. I will hurt you."

"Yeah, yeah. Get up." I let go of his hand and stretched. After he got out of the driver's side, he rushed to my side to open the door. He locked the car doors, and we made our way into our building. He walked me to my room, and we stood outside my door talking for a few minutes.

"I like you… I hope we get to the point where we really love each other. I can see myself with you", he said out of the blue. "And I'm interested in learning more about Christianity, but I just need time."

I nodded, "I understand. Like, I said I'm here. And I hope we can get to the point of loving each other, too." I smiled, and he returned it. He looked at my lips. *I know that look.* He grabbed my waist, pulling me closer to him. Doing the same thing he did when we first kissed. He took forever to actually kiss me, but instead of getting impatient this time, I did the same. We finally kissed. Each time was more magical than the last. He eventually gently backed me up against the wall. One of his hands slid up the back of my shirt while the other one found its way to my butt.

I knew I needed to stop him before things got too heated. And it would seem really hypocritical to keep teasing him like this. I was so into it, I almost lost myself. I've never wanted somebody like this. At the moment I couldn't decide if that was a good thing or not. I let his hands roam and I was starting to feel too comfortable with that.

Kyrah. Stop it. Instead of hearing my own thoughts, which were only encouraging the situation, I heard the Holy Spirit. That's when I pulled it together. I broke the kiss by slightly pushing him away.

"We should chill", I suggested while trying to catch my breath.

He nodded, "Yeah, my bad. Got too carried away." He backed up so I could move from the wall. "I'll call you tomorrow."

I smiled, "Okay. Goodnight, baby."

"Night, babygirl." He kissed my forehead and walked away. I walked in my room feeling grateful and ashamed at the same time. I went straight to my room, changed my clothes, and lied on my bed staring at the ceiling. I didn't need to see him tomorrow. I'm glad he only said he would call me and not see me. It was too risky right now. I needed time to think and get myself together. I lied in bed trying to give myself a pep talk in my head.

I can't believe I even went that far. Even though we were just kissing, it could have gone further. What is wrong with you, Kyrah? You have to be more careful. You're the example. Not him. Get it together.

I closed my eyes as tears unexpectedly slipped out. I tried to fight back the tears, but I couldn't. I felt very vulnerable. I felt guilt. And all we did was kiss. If I was feeling like this after just a passionate, intense kiss, I didn't even want to imagine how I would feel if I decided to have sex. I shook the thoughts out of my head and tried to go to sleep. This night did not go how I wanted it to.

Chapter 7

"You, Lord, are forgiving and good, abounding in love to all who call to you." (Psalm 86:5)

It had been three days since Anthony and I had our little episode. I had been avoiding him. And I think he knew that. It was wrong, I know. But the confidence I once had in being able to control myself was beginning to slip away. He's been trying to come see me and I've told him that I've been sick, I've had too much work and he's a distraction—Anything. I was running out of excuses and I knew I needed to see him. He's my boyfriend. I couldn't stay away from him. Plus, I was starting to miss him like crazy.

While I was sitting in my room, feeling restless, Anthony texted me:

I'm coming to see you. I'm not asking you this time. Lol. I miss you. :(

I smiled to myself. Although I was nervous about us being in the same room together, I knew I couldn't avoid him anymore.

Fine by me. I miss you, too... :/

We texted back and forth for a little while until he let me know he was on his way up here. About two minutes later, I heard on a knock on our door. I stayed in my room since Tamra was in the living room.

"Ky, your boyfriend's here", she yelled. I walked out of my room and motioned for him to come in my room. He met me at my door and just looked at me.

"You in trouble, I hope you know that", he said walking past me to sit in the chair at my desk.

I sighed, "Yeah, I'm aware." I closed the door and followed him further into my room.

"Why you avoiding me?" he asked leaning back. The way he was looking at me was intimidating.

I shrugged my shoulders before sitting on my bed. I met his gaze as he frowned a little bit.

"Nah, don't do that. What's wrong? What did I do?" he asked.

"You didn't do anything. I'm not worried about you. I just needed… some me time. I had to pull myself back together."

"Back together from what? You avoidin' the question" he stated slightly impatiently.

"Okay, you can calm down—"

"Nah, I'm tryna talk to you and you act like you can't give me a straight answer."

"I'm trying to answer you, if you stop talking."

"Man… I ain't come up here to argue wit' you. I'm tryna have a conversation with you and feel where you comin' from, but you always gotta get amped and sh—"

"Don't cuss at me."

He nodded before standing up. He began walking towards the door and I became even more livid than before.

"Where you going? How do you possibly start an argument and walk away?" I asked angrily.

"I'm going back to my room. Let me know when you lose the attitude."

I couldn't believe he just said that to me. He starts the argument and then walks away. He didn't kiss me or anything. He just came in ready to argue with me.

"Well, you wait for that", I replied with more attitude than I had before.

He turned around and closed the door again. I could feel this arguement getting worse from this point on.

"See, that's what I'm talking about! Your attitude, bruh… Why you can't just answer my question?"

"I was trying to, but you won't shut up! Learn to listen sometimes and let me talk! Then maybe you would know why I was avoiding you!"

He shook his head as he opened my door again and continued to walk out of my room. He closed my door, and I heard the main door close shortly after. I rolled my eyes as tears threatened to fall from my eyes. I did the best I could to keep them from falling, but I couldn't any longer. They finally flowed. It felt good, but I was mad at myself. I can't believe I let a guy bring me to tears. Suddenly, I heard a soft knock on my door. I knew it was Tamra checking on me, but I didn't want to talk right now.

"Kyrah? Are you ok?" she asked from the other side of the door.

I sniffed as tears still flowed. "I'm fine, Tam."

"You sure?"

No. "Yeah."

"Okay." With that, I lied down on my bed and let the silent tears continue to flow. I hated Anthony for making me cry like this. We've had two arguments within the last few days. I no longer knew what to do. I know couples had arguments, but I had no idea it would be like this. This was so new to me, but what hurt the most was knowing that I upset somebody that I truly cared about and was growing to love.

I cried for what felt like hours. I couldn't believe he just walked out. I didn't like this feeling. This is why I wanted to be single. None of this would be happening if I hadn't taken a chance on a guy who couldn't control his hormones and didn't know how to work out his issues. As much as I wanted to call him and go see him, I fought the urge. I wasn't going to give in. If he could play this game, I could play it better.

I decided that it would be best if I got up and went to Bible Study. I hadn't been in a few weeks because I was so busy with schoolwork, but I figured today would be a perfect day to go. I freshened up and about five minutes later, I was out the door. I avoided eye contact with Tamra because I didn't want to talk about Anthony right now. I quickly walked out of the room and headed to Bible Study.

"Is there anything you all would like us to pray for or that you're thankful for?" the group leader, Mrs. Lisa asked. People raised their hands left and right. I knew I wanted them to pray for me, but I didn't want everyone to know what was going on. I decided to wait and talk to her after we prayed. Once everyone finished putting in their prayer request, Mrs. Lisa prayed for everyone.

"In your precious Son's, Jesus's name we pray, Amen", she finished. "Alright guys, thank you all for coming. See you all next time."

I quickly got up and hurried to her so I could talk to her about my problem, aka, Anthony.

“Hey, Mrs. Lisa”, I greeted.

She looked at me with a big smile, “Hey, Kyrah! How are you?”

I shook my head and sighed, “I’m okay, I guess. I didn’t want to raise my hand during the prayer request because I’m slightly embarrassed.”

“Oh, don’t be! Come on, let’s talk about it.” We sat down in the nearest chairs across from each other. “What’s going on?”

“Well, I’ve been dating this guy for the past almost two months, and he’s a great guy. I care about him a lot. But we just got into an argument, and it was pretty bad. He’s not a Christian, but he said he’s interested in learning more about it, so I figured that was the first step. But he’s a very “touchy” person and we talked about that, which made us argue. But last time we hung out, I almost went there with him. I stopped it, and I avoided him for a few days after that. So, he came to see me today and asked me why, but he got frustrated when I wouldn’t give him the answer he wanted to hear. And now I don’t know what to do. I’m so…”, a tear slipped out of my eye, “I just don’t know. I’m so new to dating. He’s my first boyfriend and I almost feel like I don’t want to lose him. I hate that I upset him and it's driving me crazy that he's mad at me. I don't know what to do, Mrs. Lisa."

I shook my head as I wiped my eyes. I didn't mean to cry again, but I couldn't help it. Knowing that I upset the one guy I truly cared about was killing me on the inside. I hated that I felt this way about him so soon, but I couldn't fight it.

"You know, Kyrah, it's perfectly normal to feel this way. Especially after a very first fight. But you have to sit back and ask God what it is He wants you to do. Use this time of you and your boyfriend not talking to talk to God. Give it to Him. He knows better than anybody how much you care about this young man. And I'm sure he cares about you even more. If he didn't, I don't think he would be upset about this. Just give him some time and give yourself some time. Be the light in this situation. Pray for him. And you said he wasn't a Christian? This may the opportunity to show him Jesus. I don't know this young man, but hearing the way you talk about him makes me think that you're supposed to be in his life. And Kyrah, it's okay to cry."

I smiled as more tears spilled out. I hugged her while thanking her. I left the room and quickly walked back to my building. I hurried back to my room and lied back in my position on my bed. I sighed and closed my eyes. Today was possibly one of the most emotionally draining days I had ever experienced. I lied like that for hours. I was hearing what Mrs. Lisa was saying, but it was gonna take some time. I couldn't just bounce back like that. I really wanted to call him and apologize. But for what? He started it. Becoming fed up with my thoughts, I eventually pulled the covers over me and drifted into a peaceful sleep.

~~~

It's been another two days of not seeing or talking to Anthony. We couldn't both possibly be this stubborn. I hated it. I wanted to talk to him! But I refused to be the one to initiate the conversation. It was Sunday so I was stuck in my room doing nothing. Both Raynah and Tamra went home for the weekend so I was alone. Hearing my stomach growl, I figured it would be best to go to the cafeteria. I quickly put some joggers on, a pull over hoody, and my running shoes on. I put my hair up in a puff and made my way out of my room.

As I was walking to the cafeteria, I spotted Anthony looking down at his phone walking in my direction. I rolled my eyes to myself, hoping he wouldn't see me. Trying to avoid eye contact only made me meet his gaze. I quickly looked away and tried to walk past him as fast as possible.
~~~

“So, you don’t see me now?” he said as our paths met. I stopped walking and looked at him.

“Anthony, I don’t feel like it today. So, please, whatever smart comments you have, keep ‘em.” I proceeded to walk away, but he gently grabbed my wrist pulling me back towards him.

“Baby, don’t be like that—”

“I’m not being any kinda way. I just wanna go eat.”

“Well, let me take you to your favorite place. I know you can’t resist. There’s nothing in the caf, anyway.”

I rolled my eyes, “Fine. Fine.”

We walked to his car in silence. Even the car ride to Zaxby’s was in silence. And it was far from that comfortable silence from the other night. I was really upset with him. I may have missed him, but I was not happy about our current situation.

About fifteen minutes later, we arrived at Zaxby’s since it wasn’t too far from the school. He came to the passenger side and opened the door for me. He looked at me, and gave me a sincere, but saddened smiled. I returned it. We quickly went inside the restaurant, ordered our food, and found a secluded table where we could talk.

Anthony sighed, “I can’t do this.”

I frowned, almost panicking over what he was about to say. “Can’t do what?”

“Us being mad at each other.” I relaxed my face as I silently sighed in relief. I nodded in agreement. “It’s really getting to me”, he continued, “I don’t like knowing that you’re mad at me. I’m sorry, babygirl. I ain’t mean to get so upset the other day. I was already kinda mad at you for avoiding me. I guess it just all came out.”

I looked at my lap, then back at him. I felt bad for avoiding him. It was something I had to do, and I didn’t think he would understand. “I’m sorry, too.”

“Nah, you don’t owe me an apology. I wouldn’t let you talk. That was all me.”

I gave him a small smile and looked down at the table. One of the employees soon called our order number and Anthony got up to go get it. Once he sat the food on the table, we began eating in silence. I wasn’t too hungry anymore. I was feeling sad. But I couldn’t figure out why.

“I’m sorry for avoiding you. I do owe you an apology. I did it because I no longer trust myself to be alone with you. I’m very afraid and nervous of what I might do. And after our little episode in the hallway the other night, I couldn’t stop feeling bad for putting you in that position just for me to stop you. I didn’t mean to take you that far. I was just caught up. So… That's why I avoided you. I don't trust me."

I felt slightly better after apologizing. I waited for the past three days to get that off my chest and it felt good to finally say it. I had been praying and praying about what to say and how to say it. I didn't want Anthony to feel bad and take the blame for everything.

He smiled, "Well… I tried to tell you that you won't be able to control yourself around me."

I laughed, "Shut up. You get on my nerves."

He laughed, "No, for real. I understand. All you had to do was tell me and I would've given you some space. I know I come onto you strong, but I'm working on that now that I know you're not into all that."

I smiled, "Well, I appreciate that. Thank you for taking that into consideration. And I'll start dressing like a nun."

He laughed, "And I'll still have a hard time keeping my hands off you." I joined him and laughed.

For the rest of our time at Zaxby's, we talked like we hadn't talked in months, even though it had only been a few days. After about another thirty minutes, we headed back to school. He walked me back to my room, like always.

"Your roommates here?" he asked.

"Nope. I'm by myself until tomorrow."

"Okay, well, I'm a phone call away if you need some company. I mean that for real this time." I smiled and leaned up to kiss him. I missed kissing him. I missed his scent. This week of barely seeing him made me realize how much I care about him.

"Yes, sir", I said finally replying.

He smiled, "See you later." I nodded and walked in my room. I sighed realizing I had nothing to do. I decided to pamper myself. That was something I hadn't done in a while. And as tempting as it was to take Anthony up on his offer, I couldn't do it. I couldn't risk being alone with him. At least not right now…

~~~

"Girl, I feel like I haven't talked to you in ages! What's going on? How's the boyfriend?" my best friend, Alana asked. After painting my nails and doing my hair, I quickly became bored again, so I decided to call my best friend. It was so nice talking to her. I could talk to my roommates, but they didn't get me like she does. She really knows how I am around guys and how I am as a person. I would swear we were soul mates if we weren't best friends.

"Well… earlier this week, we somewhat got into it about how inappropriate he is, but we made up and I almost gave him some."
~~~

It was so silent on the line, I thought I hung up. "Lana?" I said making sure she was still there.

"Wait! You what? You almost had sex? Girl, what?!" she exclaimed. I almost laughed, but I knew she was serious.

"Yes… It was a mistake. That's why I avoided him for three days which only led to a bigger argument and us not talking for another two days. It was just… too much."

"Well, where were you guys when you almost "did it"?"

I hesitantly answered her question. I was ashamed enough, but it made it worse that it almost went down where people could accidently see.

"In the hallway right in front of my door."

"Oh my gosh… Kyrah… You freak." I cracked up. I couldn't help it. Her response was everything I needed to help lighten the situation.

"Anyway, we made up today. He took me to Zaxby's, and we sat and talked everything out. We're on a good note right now. I hope it stays that way. He offered to sit up here with me to keep my company, but I don't trust myself."

"What do you mean?"

I sighed, "I can't guarantee that what happened earlier this week won't happen again, and we won't go all the way. I have to put limitations on myself."

"Well, you gotta do what you gotta do. He'll understand. He seems like a good guy who respects you and understands."

"Yeah, I guess…"

Chapter 8

"…to be self-controlled and pure, to be busy at home, to be kind, and to be their husbands, so that no one will malign the word of God." (Titus 2:5)

It's been a few weeks since everything went down between me and Anthony. Things have been going great so far and every day, I prayed they would stay that way. It's a Monday afternoon and I'm sitting with Anthony at one of the campus restaurants. Anthony asked me if I wanted to go to this kickback in one of his friend's room with him on Friday, but I'm not a big fan of being around a lot of people. He said if I didn't want to go, he wouldn't go, but I know he wants to. I didn't want to be a buzzkill and stop his fun.

"Well, what are you gonna do if you ain't tryna go to the kickback?" he asked while we ate our food at an on-campus restaurant.

I shrugged slightly, "I'll find something to do."

He shook his head giving me the side-eye. "Man… You so stubborn."

I frowned, slightly taken aback. "Excuse me? I am not!"

He laughed, "Yes, you are. You don't wanna go to the party, so I offer to hang out with you, but you don't want me to… and now you whinin' about not having nothin' to do."

I rolled my eyes. *Okay, so maybe I am a little stubborn. So what?*

"I said I would figure something out. Don't worry about me. Go have fun." He rolled his eyes and I did it back.

"Kyrah, don't start", he warned before eating a few French fries. I playfully rolled my eyes again just get on his nerves. "Stop playin' with me, man. I'm serious about ditching the party. I wanna hang out with you."

I gave him a glare, "Anthony Jamal Wright, let it go. Go to the party. Have fun."

"Kyrah Michelle Brown, no, I will not. Now stop telling me what I'm gon' do. If I wanna hang out with my babygirl, I will."

I smirked and admired him as he continued eating his food. I love every bit of Anthony's personality. I love how he talked to me, it was both romantic and flirtatious, but also assertive with respect. I love how he talked about me. I love how he looks at me. I love how he wants to prove his love for me in every way but controls himself out of respect for me. We may have our differences, but I feel like our chemistry is real. I love him… Yeah, that's it. I love him. But I wasn't sure if I could tell him. My thoughts were interrupted when I saw him look at me and smile.

"What?" he said.

I shook my head lightly, "No-nothing… I was just thinking about something."

He raised one eyebrow, but eventually just nodded and let it go. We soon finished eating and left the restaurant. I walked back to my room alone since he had another class. As I was walking, I noticed some girls staring at me and whispering to one another. I frowned as I kept walking. They eventually started following me which weirded me out a little bit. I stopped walking and turned around.

"Can I help you with something?" I asked in the nicest way possible [which still came off pretty rude. I'm a blunt person, I can't help it.].

"Oh, aren't you Anthony Wright's girlfriend?" one of the girls asked.

"I might be. Why?"

"Oh, no reason. I was just… curious."

I nodded my head slowly, still frowning out of aggravation and confusion. "Okay… Well, nice to meet you, I guess."

"Mmhm, you too." She winked and walked away. That girl and her friends rubbed me the wrong way. Who just randomly walks up to someone and gets all in their business? Who was she to ask me who I'm dating? I don't even know her! And the last thing I needed was for some random to start spreading rumors about me. My school was not that big, but it was big enough for people to mind their business. I pulled out my phone and searched Anthony's name.

We need to talk. Call me or come see me after class.

I didn't even wait for him to respond. I just put my phone in my back pocket and proceeded to my room. I was so thrown off by the way those girls approached me, I wasn't even sure what I needed to talk to Anthony about.

I was sitting in the living room of my dorm working on a paper. I decided to do some work to keep me from becoming so anxious and impatient while waiting for Anthony. He replied just saying "Ok, baby". His response made me a little less worried, but I was still somewhat on edge, nonetheless. I constantly repeated the scene with those girls in my head. What did they want with me? Interrupting my thoughts, I heard a knock on the door. I placed my computer down and hurried to the door. I figured it was Anthony, so I just opened the door. And I was right.

"Hey, bae, what's going on? Are you okay?" he asked worried. I gave a small smile at how concerned he was.

"Yeah, I'm fine. I just wanted to talk to you about the weirdest thing that happened after we parted ways earlier." I opened the door wider for him to come in. He followed me to couch, and we sat down. He patted his lap for me to put my feet in. *He's so sweet...* I placed my feet in his lap, and he smiled.

"A'ight, so what happened?" he asked.

"Okay, these girls, it was three of them. They were, like, following me. So, I turned around and was like, 'Can I help you?' and they were just like, 'You're Anthony Wright's girlfriend?' and I just said, 'I might be. Why?' So, she was just like, 'No reason, just wondering.' And I said it was nice to meet her and I walked away. I wish I had gotten a picture so you could see her. You may know her. I just thought it was weird."

I looked at him and he just had his eyebrows raised.

"Isn't that weird?" I asked.

He chuckled, "Yeah, babe, but you're worried about that?"

I rolled my eyes, “Yeah! These girls were following me. Who knows if they were plotting to jump me or something? Like how does she know me? Plus, I figured you might know her.”

“Well, what she look like?”

“The girl that did all the talking was sorta light skinned, really cute short cut, lips kinda big, dark brown eyes, and she was kinda short, too. Really cute girl.”

He nodded and let out deep sigh. “Erica…”

“Erica? So, you do know her?”

He looked at me and nodded. He had an almost painful look on his face, “Yeah. We… Messed around. We were never exclusive, though.”

I looked down at my lap, “Oh…”

That wasn’t exactly what I wanted to hear. Of course, I should’ve expected it, but I didn’t. I wasn’t sure what was going to come out of his mouth. It most certainly wasn’t that. I knew there had to be a good reason that girl—Erica was following me around. Suddenly, I was starting feel competitive and sad. I couldn’t really explain how I was feeling even if I knew. I almost felt like I was no longer good enough for Anthony. Insecure. That’s the word. That’s what his confession made me feel.

"Babe?" he said snapping me out my thoughts.

I looked at him, holding back tears. I kept hoping that it wasn't obvious I was trying not to cry. I was starting to feel that being with Anthony brought nothing but tears.

"Y-yeah?" I finally answered.

"Did you hear me?" I shook my head no.

"I asked if you're okay. You mad?"

I shrugged, and tried to swallow my tears away, "About what? It's not like you're messing around with her now. That was before me."

He nodded and grabbed my hand, softly caressing it with his thumb. "You know I can see right through you, right? I know you're upset."

I shook my head and looked back at my lap. A tear managed to escape my eyes. *Damn it...* I quickly wiped it away. Anthony gently placed his hand under my chin and made me look at him.

"What you cryin' for?" he asked.

"I don't know. I guess I just wasn't expecting that. I mean, duh, you're not a virgin, but it's weird to picture you with another girl... Because she gave you something I haven't."

He gently removed my feet from his lap and held out his arms for me to cuddle in. I moved closer to him until his arms were completely around me. I rested my head on his shoulder and let my tears escape.

"You shouldn't feel anything about that. Don't worry about her and what we did. Me and you, we good. I'm not checking for her anymore. I'm with you. I only want you. Don't trip about saving yourself. That's cool with me. A'ight?"

I just nodded in response so he would stop talking about what he and Erica did together. For some reason, his little reassurance didn't really help. Just knowing that he was only a hook up buddy with some girl made me sick my stomach. It wasn't making me question our relationship in any way, shape, or form. But unfortunately, it was making me question my decision to make him wait. I know he said he was okay with that, but I suddenly wasn't. I felt like I had to compete with Erica and the only thing that I can compete with is the fact that she gave herself to him. And I knew it was wrong for me to even be questioning my purity and my decision to do God's Will, but what else was I supposed to do?

"A'ight, well, I'ma go. Or do you want me to stay?" he asked before he moved.

"No, you don't have to stay. I need to some work, anyway. You're a distraction."

He gave a hearty laugh that I could feel in his chest. I smiled.

"Okay, well, get to work. I'll leave. Gimme kiss."

I looked up at his puckered lips and kissed them. I sat up so he could get up from the couch.

"I'll talk to you later." He leaned down and kissed my forehead. I nodded and watched him walk out of the door. I sighed. I couldn't believe I was considering actually sleeping with Anthony. It was idiotic, I know, but I wanted to do everything I could to keep him. I sat on the couch in one position for a while telling myself how stupid I am.

Suddenly, the door flew open and in walked Tamra. She looked at me with a smile.

"Hey, girl! What you doin' out here?" she asked as she plopped beside me.

"That party this Friday… We should go," I blurted out. I needed to get out and stop thinking so much. I knew Anthony was still going, but that's not why I wanted to go. I wanted to let go. I'm always so worried. Maybe that'll help me stop thinking about compromising myself.

Tamra looked at me as if she had just seen a ghost. She quickly smiled, "Don't mess with me right now, Kyrah. Did you just say you wanted to go to a party?"

I quickly nodded my head, "Yeah. Let's do it. I need to go have some fun. I feel overwhelmed and I just wanna not think about anything other than looking cute for one night."

She nodded with a huge smile on her face, "Oh, hell yeah! We doin' this! You don't know how much you just made my day. I gotta tell Ray when she gets back." I laughed at her excitement. I never thought I would be the one suggesting going to a party, but this was just what I needed to get my mind off Erica, my crazy thoughts, and even Anthony. It was time I had some fun…

The rest of the week sort of dragged by. I finished my paper a whole week ahead of time, so I had extra free time. I spent a lot of time mentally preparing myself to be bombarded with a bunch of strangers at this party. By the time Thursday rolled around, I was beginning to regret bringing it up. I just wanted to sit in my room and mope and watch movies all weekend. But Tamra was really looking forward to it, and now that I told Anthony, he kind of was too. So now I felt like I had to go.

As I was on the way to my room from my last class, I saw Erica walking by herself. I avoided eye contact with her so she wouldn't say anything to me.

"Hey!" she called as I was just passing her. *Ugh! What do you want?!* As tempting as it was to be rude and just keep walking, I decided to practice being Christ-like. I put on a fake smile and looked at her.

"Hi...," I replied in the nicest way possible.

"How's Anthony?"

I frowned slightly taken aback. *I know this heffa did not just ask about my boyfriend.* "Um, why?"

She gave a sly smirk, "Oh, I'm sorry. You don't want me asking about your boyfriend?"

"What do you want? Why are you suddenly bothering me?"

She moved a little closer, but I backed up with one clenched fist. That was my personal warning for her not to move any closer. I was not in the mood to deal with anybody's BS, especially not some chick's I didn't even know. She held her hands up in a surrendering motion and backed up.

"I just want warn you that you might want to know that he was in my room last night, and... Let's just say, we did more than just talk." I looked at her, becoming even more annoyed. I was afraid that if I kept looking at her, I might seriously hurt her. Instead, I just nodded.

I cleared my throat, "Thanks for letting me know that irrelevant information. Now if you don't mind, I would like to go to my room in peace."

She shrugged, "Just thought you should know. See ya 'round." She winked and walked away. *That damn winking!* I hated her and I didn't even know her. But did I really need to? She was basically showing me what kind of person she was. I proceeded to walk to my room as tears started forming. I wiped my eyes, but they just kept coming. As I was walking through the door, I saw Anthony coming. I rolled my eyes, and wiped my eyes before he could see me. The security guard wasn't present, so I just kept walking.

"Hey, babygirl", he greeted with a smile. I looked at him and sort of smiled.

He quickly frowned, "Woah, woah! You crying? What's going on? You okay?"

I put on a fake smile, "I'm fine. I need to get to my room. I'll talk to you later." I proceeded to walk away, leaving Anthony standing there.

"Wait, Kyrah!" he called. I ignored him and kept walking to the elevator. Tears kept flowing. I couldn't stop them. I kept pushing the elevator button until it finally made it to the first floor. It was obvious Anthony didn't care that much. He would've chased after me. As soon as I reached my dorm, I quickly hurried to my room. I closed the door and locked it. I dropped my things and let the tears freely flow. Being in a relationship with Anthony has really made me feel things I don't like. I wasn't used to this. And for the first time since we had been together, I wanted out. If what Erica was saying was true, I definitely didn't want any part of this relationship. But was it really logical for me to believe some random girl? However, the part that worried me the most was the fact that I didn't care if she was lying or not. I had never cried so much until I got in a relationship with him.

Being with him was starting to hurt me more than anything. And it's not his fault because he doesn't know I'm feeling like this. I won't tell him. I can't. It would hurt him. I slowly sat on my bed and cried my eyes out. A part of me was pretty sure Erica was lying, but another part of me actually believed her. The rest of me just didn't care and wanted to break things off with Anthony. I didn't like that part of me. There was a knock on my door that shook me out of my crying and my thoughts.

"Babygirl?" I heard Anthony call through the door. I quickly looked up and sighed. *So, he followed me...* I hadn't even heard him come in. I guess I was crying too much. "Kyrah, open the door, baby", he called again.

Finally standing up, I unlocked my door and opened it. I no longer cared about the fact that I had tears streaming down my face.

"Why aren't you in class?" I asked harsher than I intended to.

"Woah, chill. I skipped. I came to check on you. What's wrong?"

I sighed as another tear slipped, "Sorry. I just… I don't know."

"Come on, let's sit down", he suggested. He moved closer into my room and closed my door, locking it shortly after. We both sat on my bed in silence for a minute. I continued to let the tears flow. I didn't even know I could cry this much.

"You gotta talk to me. I can't help you if you don't. That's what's wrong. I know we haven't been together that long, but don't you trust me? You have to let me in. Talk to me, baby", he said breaking the silence.

I hesitated to say anything, but I finally did. "That girl… Erica. She told me that you were in her room last night and you guys did more than just talk. So, I got upset."

He frowned, "You believe her?"

I shrugged, shaking my head, "I don't know." I wiped eyes suddenly wishing I wouldn't have said that. *Now he's going to think I don't trust him.*

He nodded. I felt his mood changing. "I guess you don't trust me."

"Anthony, don't—"

"Nah, it's cool. You don't have to worry about it. It's cool. I'm actually cool on you." He stood up and walked towards the door.

"See, that's why I don't talk to you! 'Cause you always walking away! You don't listen to me and I wish you'd stop doing that!" I yelled. I was fed up.

"Look, shawty—"

"Shawty? It's like that? So that's all I am to you now?"

He shrugged, "Yeah, it's just like that. I'll see you around." And with that, he opened my door, leaving me sitting on the bed in shock. I thought I would have run out of tears by now, but more came pouring out of my eyes. I couldn't control them. I couldn't understand what just happened. I looked up to see Tamra standing in my doorway.

"Are you ok?" she asked.

I shrugged, "I don't know. I guess I got what I wanted." She came and sat beside and turned towards me.

"Who is Erica? Start there", she asked.

"The girl Anthony used to mess with before me. She's bothered me twice this week about him and today she told me that they did some stuff in her room last night. The only reason I somewhat believed her is because I'm not… Wasn't going to have sex with him. And I figured she gave him something I wasn't willing to."

She nodded, "I'm sorry, Kyrah. He should've just listened to you."

I rolled my eyes, "It's whatever. I'm tired of crying. I just wanna sleep."

She chuckled, "Okay. Well, you need all the rest you can get so we can go turn up tomorrow. And now that you just had a big thing with Anthony, you need it." As much as I wanted to object and convince her to let me stay in my bed and mope around, she was right. This break up or whatever we just had gave me another reason to go have fun. And that's what I intended to do…

Chapter 9

"Do not get drunk on wine, which leads to debauchery. Instead, be filled with the Spirit, ..." (Ephesians 5:18)

Friday night. 8:00 p.m., to be exact. And I was ready to go have fun. I tried as hard as I could to keep my mind off Anthony, and so far, it was working. I finished touching up my makeup and decided to wear my hair in my big curly afro. I put on a black fitted skirt, a black crop top, and some black Converses. Tamra walked out her room and saw me. She smiled and snapped her fingers.

"Girl, I swear… If I were a boy, I would be tryna holla' at you. Yaasss, boo!" she said looking me up and down like she was impressed.

I smiled and winked, "Thanks, girl! I try, I try."

I was happy Tamra didn't bring up anything from yesterday. She allowed me to sulk and get myself back together. One thing about me, I know how to bounce back. It was much easier than I imagined. However, I felt like it wouldn't last long.

By the time 9:00 rolled around, we were all ready. I couldn't help but be amused at how excited

Tamra and Raynah were about me going to a party. Honestly, I was excited myself. This would be my first party and I was really looking forward to it. We quickly arrived at the 12-bedroom suite that the party was being held in. When we walked in, my stomach began to feel funny. I saw Anthony. He saw me. We locked eyes for a brief moment. I quickly looked away and turned to listen to what Tamra was saying.

"Okay, guys. Let's turn up!" she exclaimed. I smiled as we walked deeper into the room. There was a lot of people in here, which I expected. But it wasn't as overwhelming as I thought it would be. Finally finding a comfortable spot to stand in, I observed everyone. Some people were very entertaining. Suddenly, I heard "Fight Night" by Migos come on. I immediately wanted to start dancing, but I held my composure.

"Excuse me, beautiful", a heard a voice say from beside me. I looked to see who it was. It was a really cute light skinned guy with dreads, dimples, and one of the prettiest smiles I had ever seen. He was pretty good looking, but he wasn't Anthony. I had seen him around but never really paid him any attention.

"Yes?" I answered, flashing him a smile.

"I was wondering if you wanted to dance."

I hesitated to give him an answer. I looked at Anthony who was looking dead at me. He quickly turned his head when I met his gaze. I rolled my eyes and gave my attention back to pretty boy.

I smiled, “Sure.” He smiled even wider, holding out his hand for me to grab. By the time we started dancing, it was already on Quavo’s verse. It was weird being this close to another guy. I wasn’t sure if I liked it, but I tried not to think about it too much. I didn’t do much, we just went with the flow. It was nice to be noticed, though. The song ended and we stopped dancing.

“What’s your name?” he asked as he got closer to my ear.

“Kyrah. Yours?”

“I’m Jesse.”

I smiled, “Pleasure to meet you.”

“Pleasure’s all mine, sweetheart. Thanks for dancing with me.” He kissed my cheek and we walked back to where I was standing before. “Can I get you something to drink?” he asked. *My mom always told me not to take drinks from strangers. But he’s such a nice guy... But I don’t know him. Maybe I-*

“She good”, I heard a familiar voice say before I could answer. Jesse put his hands up as if he was surrendering.

“Yo, my bad. I’ll see you around, beautiful.”

“Nah, you won’t. But thanks for keeping her company”, Anthony said. I rolled my eyes. I was so over his mood swings. I could have sworn he broke up with me the day before. Jesse shrugged and walked away. I crossed my arms and gave Anthony a frown.

He looked at me and smirked, “You’re welcome.”

“Keep it. I didn’t ask you to do that. You were just jealous.”

He scoffed, “Baby, I don’t get jealous. You just looked uncomfortable.”

I shook my head in disbelief. “Anthony, you either want to be with me or you don’t. But since we’re no longer together, I don’t need you to come save me or whatever you think you’re doing from other guys. He was being nice. Something you should try. So please, leave me alone.” I gave him one last look and went to go stand with Tamra. She was standing next to the punch bowl, so I decided to get some. I had a weird feeling about drinking anything from this party, but I figured I was just being paranoid. After taking the first sip, I decided that this was the best punch I’d ever had. *This is so good... Omg.* I downed the rest of the punch and went back for more. After the fourth cup, I started feeling funny. I figured it was time to chill on the drink and go have fun.

"Tam! Let's dance!" I yelled. I didn't know what came over me. I was feeling loose. Freer. I didn't want to lose this feeling. I grabbed Tamra's hands and dragged her to the middle of the floor. We danced and danced. Next thing I knew, I was dancing with another guy. I hadn't even realized that he was being inappropriate with the way he was touching my butt. I was having too much fun to care. Eventually, I came to my senses and moved his hands off of me. I looked at his face with blurred vision not sure who I was looking at. He smiled and continued to grab me.

"Can you stop?" I asked, starting to feel lightheaded.

"Come on, baby. Don't be like that", the random guy said pulling me closer. I began to feel a panic in my chest.

I pushed him off again, "Stop!" Out of nowhere, I felt gentle hands on my waist from behind pull me away from the guy. I saw Anthony step in front of me and get in the guy's face.

"Ay, bruh. She said stop. Chill out", he said calmly.

The random guy scoffed, "What you gon' do? We were havin' a good time. Weren't we, baby?" he asked me as he tried to peek at me. Before I could open my mouth to say anything, Anthony looked me as if to tell me not to say anything.

"You don't wanna know what I'ma do. But if you keep bothering her, you gon' find out. Now I said chill out." Everyone in the room stopped to see the drama happening in the middle of the floor and I was annoyed. *This is why I should've stayed in my room... What was I thinking?* The random guy chuckled and surrendered his hands.

"You got it, bruh. I ain't fightin' over no bitch", he said. Anthony faked like he was about to turn around and before I knew it, his fist connected to the guy's jaw. My mouth flew open. Two other guys came in and tried to break them up. By this time, the whole suite was in an uproar. Tamra and Raynah came by my side and pulled me away from the commotion. I began to feel lightheaded again as I was looking around. My vision was becoming blurry again.

"Kyrah? Kyrah! Are you okay?" Raynah kept asking me. I looked at her and shook my head.

"I don't feel so well..." was the last thing I said before everything went black.

I opened my eyes, not knowing where I was. I noticed that it was the next day. I lied there trying to figure out when I fell asleep and why I was still in my clothes from the night before. I tried to sit up, but the worst pain in my head arose. I closed my eyes from the excruciating sensation. Suddenly, I felt movement in the bed from another person.

"Don't move too fast. Here, drink some water", Anthony said as he came to my side. *What's he doing here?* I sat up slowly, still feeling the hammering inside of my brain. I took the bottled water from Anthony and drank it. After a few sips, I looked at him.

"What happened?" I asked.

"You got drunk and passed out."

I frowned, "How did I get drunk? I didn't drink anything other than punch."

He smirked, "Somebody spiked it. It was barely punch. How much did you drink?"

I rubbed my head trying to ease the pain. I know he was talking really low, but it felt like he was yelling. "I don't know. Three? Four cups? I don't remember. It was good. I thought it was a special punch."

He laughed, "It was definitely a special punch." I laughed with him. It became silent for a moment. I looked at him and noticed his busted lip and a few scratches on his face. I frowned and reached up to touch him.

"Your face…" I said suddenly feeling guilty. I remember everything that happened right before I passed out. A guilty feeling then came over me. He touched my hand and shook his head.

“Don’t worry about me, babygirl. Are you okay, though?” he asked sincerely.

“Yeah, I’m fine. I’m mad at you, though.”

He frowned, “I know.”

“Why did you fight that guy? You could get kicked out. You can’t be doing stuff like, Anthony. You can’t leave me.”

He looked down for a second, then looked back at me. “I had to. He could’ve hurt you. You’re worth getting kicked out over.” I shook my head as more guilt sank in. I hated that he got into a fight because of me. I hated that I even went to that party. None of this would have happened if I had just stayed in my room.

“I guess the only good thing that came out of this is us talking…” I blurted out.

He nodded, “True. I missed you… Even though it was only a day.”

“One day too long.” I looked down as a tear slipped out. I had to admit, I did miss him. Although it wasn’t that long, it was sort of torturous. I was honest about being able to bounce back, but I honestly didn’t want to. Last night was fun up to a certain point, and it did help me get my mind off Anthony and our breakup.

But I still missed him. I wanted to hold him and admit that I love him. But I wasn't sure if I could take him back after he just blew me off. What if he did it again?

"What are you thinking about?" Anthony asked interrupting my thoughts.

I sighed inwardly before speaking. "I miss you", I began hesitantly, "but… I don't know. Part of me wants us to get back together, and the other part of me thinks this is for the best."

"What do you mean? You don't want to get back together?"

"That's the thing, I don't know. How do I know you won't just blow me off again over something so small? You don't listen to me when I try to open up to you. You didn't even try to understand why I somewhat believed Erica."

He stood up and sat on the bed where my feet were. "Kyrah, there is no reason you should believe some random girl before hearing what your boyfriend has to say."

"She's not just some random girl, Anthony, and you know that. Whether you want to admit it or not, you two have history. Now she may have been confused about what it was between you guys, but it's obvious some kind of feelings were involved. She was able to give you something I'm not willing to give you, yet.

That's why I almost believed her. I just thought maybe you would find pleasure elsewhere. It's stupid, I know… I just…" I sighed while shaking my head. The tears finally stopped so I was able to talk without feeling overly vulnerable.

Finally looking at Anthony, I saw the hurt in his eyes. That was the last thing I wanted to do. I didn't mean for my words to hurt him, but that's truly how I felt. I felt insecure. Being with Anthony was intimidating. He's an intimidating guy. He had plenty of girls that wanted to be with him because he's so attractive. He's beautiful. Breathtaking. And trying to understand how we ended up together in the first place is something I can't quite figure out.

"Baby… I'm not trying to be with anybody else. You don't understand how much I admire you as a person, as a woman. You give me hope for my future. I see myself with you. I've never met anybody strong enough to save themselves for someone they don't even know. Even when you're tempted, you still remain strong. I admire how you look at life. I admire how positive you are. I even admire your relationship with God. I started reading an old Bible I had that collected dust." He chuckled. "I've learned so much about God and who He is because of you. You… I have to believe God sent you to me. I even think I'm ready to accept Jesus in my heart."

I looked at him as my eyes lit up. I smiled, “Really, Anthony? That’s beautiful! I’m so happy for you!”

He smiled, “Yeah. But babygirl, you can’t… I need you. I gotta have you with me. We have to stay together. I feel like we’re supposed to be together. I don’t know how I get that from us only dating for a short period of time, but I guess I just feel it. I’m sorry for not listening to you. I’m trying. I’m just not used to a girl being so bluntly honest with me. But I need it. I need you. Please, forgive me.”

At that moment, all the doubts I had about us being together vanished. I could easily feel peace from the Holy Spirit. I tried to lean in to kiss Anthony, but I felt the banging in my head from moving too fast. I rubbed my head, and he laughed. He then leaned in to kiss me instead. This kiss was much more innocent. Not as lustful. Something I had never felt, and I loved it. We parted and looked at one another.

“I… I love you”, I blurted out. I wasn’t sure if I meant to, but I had been waiting to say that. It felt good to finally be able to say it.

“I love you”, he responded.

Chapter 10

"On reaching the place, he said to them, "Pray that you will not fall into temptation." (Luke 22:40)

Things between Anthony and I were going beyond great. He started attending Bible Study with me and gave his life to Christ. I was proud of him. It had been a few weeks since the party and since we made up. Not to mention, today's our six-month anniversary. We decided to just chill in his room, order some Chinese takeout and watch movies for our special day. We figured that celebrating four months was not that ideal to go all out for.

"Kyrah, you're the first girl I've met that prefers comedy over romance. That's unheard of", Anthony said as he played a movie on Netflix.

I laughed, "I like to laugh, obviously."

"Yeah, I know. So silly, man", he replied smiling while looking at me. I smiled at him, then stuck my tongue out at him. I thought about the last time I did that and prayed that his reaction would be different.

He chuckled while shaking his head, “Don’t do that… For my sake. I’m tryna do better. You not makin’ it easy.”

I giggled, “Aw, I’m sorry. Okay. I’ll be more mindful of that.”

He laughed, “I greatly appreciate it.” I laughed with him as we both got comfortable. We weren’t cuddled up because we were both too busy chowing down our food. After we finished watching our comedy, we watched an action movie. I like action movies, but I let Anthony choose that one since I chose the first one. We cuddled up for this movie. I lied my head on his shoulder while his arms were wrapped around me, as he caressed my leg. I know he was doing it subconsciously, but I was tempted to tell him to stop although I somewhat wanted him to keep going. I sighed and continued to try to concentrate on the movie.

“You a’ight, babygirl?” he asked.

I nodded, “Yeah, I’m fine,” I lied.

I smiled as we kept watching the movie. I noticed that he would keep doing it and then stop. I wasn’t sure if he kept catching himself or if he was doing it torture me. I tried to focus on the movie, but the more I tried, the more I failed to actually do so.

I cleared my throat suddenly trying to distract my mind from what was happening. "I thought you were trying to do better?" I nervously joked.

"What you mean?" He asked slightly confused.

"You keep rubbing my thigh," I said with w slight chuckle.

I felt a light chuckle come from his chest. "I really am trying to keep it together… but wit' you lookin' how you lookin', that's kinda hard to do." We sat in silence for a minute. My heart began to beat faster as I was becoming more and more nervous. *Okay, now is the time to get up and move. Leave the room. Get away from Anthony.* I literally felt the Holy Spirit prompting me to move, but my flesh was starting to take over. I tried to get up, but I couldn't bring myself to do it. The more I sat there, the further away the voice was, and I suddenly couldn't hear Him anymore.

Anthony eventually stopped rubbing my leg and I looked up at him as a reaction. He leaned down to kiss me and I almost immediately kissed him back. Eventually he kissed me on the neck. I gasped a little as I closed my eyes.

"Anthony…", I said almost in a whisper.

"Hmm?" he responded, his voice deeper than before. My insides instantly melted.

"Maybe we shouldn't-"

"Just let me know when you want me to stop", he interrupted me as he kept kissing me. I was beginning to hate myself for still sitting in the same spot. But now I couldn't move. I was stuck. We suddenly shifted and I ended up on his lap. *Kyrah... Kyrah...* I suddenly heard the Holy Spirit again. We started kissing passionately, and although I knew it was going downhill from here, I started to really get into it without thinking twice about it. I could feel my heart breaking. I could feel God's disappointment and we hadn't even gone that far.

Anthony moved from my lips back to my neck. I closed my eyes suddenly feeling like I was in complete bliss. *Why does this feel so good?* He stopped all of a sudden. I slowly opened my eyes to meet his, full of lust.

He smirked, "You wanna stop?" His voice was abnormally deeper. ~~I liked it.~~ No, I loved it. *Of course, my spirit wants to stop... But phycially, I can't.* I bit my bottom lip slightly as I shook my head "no".

He nodded, "A'ight. Let's go to my room." I got off his lap as he grabbed a hold of one of my hands. He led me to his room and closed the door. After he locked it, he sat on the bed with his eyes still on me.

He grabbed my hand and slowly pulled me closer to stand between his legs.

"You sure you wanna do this?" he asked sincerely. I nodded too fast. I didn't even think about it. He smirked as he leaned in to kiss me. Now I knew there was no turning back…

I woke up in the middle of the night with Anthony's arms still wrapped around me. Wishing I was still asleep, the guilt immediately began to set in my heart. In my Spirit. I quickly closed my eyes hoping this was a dream. But I wasn't that naïve. I knew it wasn't a dream. And I couldn't even blame Anthony. He asked me if I was sure about having sex with him, and I did it anyway. I slowly sat up, being careful not to wake him up. I sighed as I looked at my hands in my lap. I looked down at my body. Nakedness under his bed sheets. Shame. Is this what Adam and Eve felt like when they sinned against God for the very first time? Well, if so, this feeling sucked. I wanted to cry, but I knew that would wake Anthony up and I knew it would probably make him feel bad. The last thing I wanted to do was make him feel like it was all his fault.

I suddenly felt movement in the bed and heard Anthony's light snore stop.

“Hey, you okay? Are you hurting?” he asked sleepily. *In more ways than you could ever imagine…*

Feeling tears form, I decided that I should probably go to my room. I blinked away the tears, faked a yawn and wiped my eyes. I looked at him and gave him a fake smile.

“Yeah, a little bit. I’m fine.”

He rolled his eyes as he sat up, “You gon’ stop lying to me. Quit tryna fool yourself like I don’t know you. What’s wrong?”

“Anthony… I need to go. Can I just go to my room?”

He sighed, giving me a long look. “Yeah, I’ll walk you back—”

“No, it’s fine. I can go by myself.”

He smacked his lips and frowned. I already knew what was about to happen. I didn’t feel like arguing with him. The tears that I tried to make disappear eventually came back.

“There you go… Pushing me away…”

“I’m not trying to push you away, Anthony. Please, just let me go. Where are my clothes?”

“I don’t know. Find them.” I shook my head in response as tears spilled out of my eyes. He was being a jerk. This is what I was trying to avoid. We wouldn’t be having this disagreement if I hadn't given him what he wanted all along. I looked at him in disbelief as he closed his eyes to go back to sleep.

Slowly getting off the bed, I found my tank top, undergarments, and sweatpants. I quickly slipped them on, all while trying to keep from crying. My pain was a mixture of hurt and disappointment.

"Bye, Anthony", I said while sniffing.

"Bye. I'll call ya." He wouldn't even look at me. I rolled my eyes as more tears surfaced. I hurried out of his room and into the living room to grab my phone, shoes, keys, and charger. As soon as I walked out of his suite, I hurried to get to my room. Remembering that it was the middle of the night, I peacefully walked into my individual room and locked the door.

Tears continuously rolled down my cheeks as I sat on the bed. My heart was broken in many ways. And it wasn't because of Anthony, but because of me. I couldn't believe I had just had sex with someone who wasn't my husband. How could I do that to my husband? To Anthony? To me? To God? I began to weep. I was hurt. Anthony giving me the cold shoulder only made it worse, but I couldn't blame him. I kicked my shoes off and lied down. I couldn't even stop crying. I always figured that having sex would bring emotional consequences, but I had no idea it would be this bad. I closed my eyes, as I drifted into a deep, but painful sleep…

I woke up to the sun shining in my face. Feeling a headache coming on, I groaned. I got out of my bed and looked at myself in the mirror. Although it wasn't physically obvious that I had given myself to Anthony, I could see it. I saw nothing but disgust and shame and guilt when I looked in the mirror. Tears began to escape my already puffy eyes. I decided to stop torturing myself and move away from the mirror. It was too much to bear. I kept having flashbacks of last night. I will admit, it was enjoyable. Very enjoyable. And although he was gentle, it still hurt a little and I was definitely feeling it. But the spiritual pain was what hurt the most. I couldn't even bring myself to talk to God. I was way too ashamed and afraid that He no longer wanted to talk to me.

After crying for another minute, I figured a shower would be a good place for me to think. Once I finished my shower, I dressed in some lounging clothes. After finally finishing getting ready, I sat on my bed and stared at my phone. *12:00 p.m.* Anthony said he would call. I know he was mad at me, but I didn't think he would not call me. And I know he wasn't still asleep. I sighed and threw my phone on my bed. What was the point of sitting here waiting for him to call when he was mad at me anyway? Part of me was feeling like I was overreacting, and another part of me felt like he was just like all the guys I'd always heard about. He got what he wanted, and now it's over.

I heard a soft knock on my door, thankfully, interrupting my overthinking.

"Come in", I said noticing how weak my voice was. The door slowly opened and in came Tamra.

"Hey…" she greeted. I gave a sad smile and waved.

"What's wrong?" she asked concerned. I hesitated. *Should I tell her? It's not really any of her business. But she's my closest friend here. I feel like I should. Maybe I'll wait. She'll probably figure it out, anyway.*

I shrugged, "Nothing. Allergies. I'm okay."

She gave me a skeptical look, "You're lying, but I'll let it slide for now. Anthony's here." I just nodded in response, although I was definitely relieved on the inside. We needed to talk. She smiled and walked out of my room. Slowly standing up, I groaned in discomfort. I slowly walked in the living room and found Anthony sitting on the couch playing with his phone.

"Hey…" I greeted. I couldn't stop my voice from sounding so weak. It was obvious I had been crying. I couldn't even hide it.

"Hey, boo" he replied. I finally made my way to the couch and sat next to him. "You in pain?" he asked sincerely.

I nodded, "Yeah, just a little. I'm okay." He nodded and looked back at his phone. I found it strange that he wasn't paying me much attention, but I still blamed myself for overreacting.

"I wasn't expecting to see you," I stated finally getting his attention.

He shrugged and smirked a little, "Just came to check on you real quick since you kinda just left last night, but I actually have to go. I'll call you later, though." He leaned over to peck me on my cheek and quickly hurried out of the door. I frowned in confusion. *What was that all about?* Tamra soon appeared from the around the corner and sat beside me. I knew what she was waiting for and I figured I might as well go ahead and tell her.

"You have sixty seconds before I beat it out of you", she threatened.

I rolled my eyes, "Okay, okay… Jeez." I sat and tried to find the words.

"We…" I drifted off and bit my bottom lip.

I looked down at my feet and waited for her to catch the hint. Hearing her gasp, I looked back at her to find her mouth wide open and her eyes big.

"You didn't…"

I nodded my head in shame. "We did…"

"Kyrah… No! I was rooting for you—"

"Tam, you're really not helping how I feel. I already feel bad enough. And don't even blame Anthony. I could've stopped him if I really wanted to…"

"And you didn't want him to?" I shook my head "no" as a sigh escaped my lips.

"Not at the time. I don't know what happened. I just became… Weak, all of a sudden. I didn't want him to stop touching me. He even asked me if I was sure I wanted to, and I didn't even think about it. I just said yes, and I couldn't turn back after that. And now I'm dealing with guilt, shame, and a light pain in my lower region."

She chuckled, "Well, at least you're taking responsibility for your part. I'm sorry that happened to you, though. I don't know… Anthony is just…" She drifted off and looked at me. I nodded knowing exactly what she meant.

"Maybe he's not good for you right now. I know I hyped it up when you guys first started dating, but I honestly can't help but blame him for this. I get it, he's your first everything, now. You almost got hurt at that damn party, and you cry all the time. And now… you've compromised yourself for him. You hardly even go to Bible Study anymore and I don't hear you talk about God that much anymore. You're different. So, no, I don't blame you. I do blame him. Even though you have a mind of your own, you can't deny that he's had some influence on you. I'm not telling you to break up with him… But I am suggesting you really take some time and decide if all of this is worth it", she finished.

I looked at my lap, contemplating what she just said. She was right. He'll never understand how this feels. He's so used to having sex with anything that has legs, and I guess he expected me to handle this a lot easier. I was beginning to question our relationship. I was even questioning his newfound salvation. Did he really accept Jesus for himself, or for me? Had I drifted so far away from God that I don't even hear Him anymore and missed all of His warnings?

Chapter 11

"It is because of Him that you are in Christ Jesus, who has become for us wisdom from God—that is, our righteousness, holiness, and redemption." (1 Corinthians 1:30)

It was Friday and I decided to go home for the weekend. Anthony and I barely talked the whole week. This time, we were avoiding each other. I wasn't entirely okay with that, but it didn't bother me like it should have. I was still thinking about what Tamra said and how right she was. I had a strange feeling in my gut telling me that he was up to no good, but I figured I'm probably being paranoid. This was probably the first time I had seen him all week. It disappointed me that he didn't really make an effort to see how I was doing, but I kept brushing off the feeling.

"This all your stuff?" Anthony asked as he picked up two of my bags.

"Yep." He nodded as we headed out of the door. Once I locked the door to my room, we left. Our walk was way too quiet for us to not have seen nor really talked to one another all week. The way he was acting towards me was really annoying me. I tried not to show it on my face since he was helping me take my stuff to my car, but it's how I feel. Once we reached my car, we packed all of my luggage into the trunk. I looked at him after everything was settled.

"Thanks for helping me with my things", I said.

"Yeah, no problem", he responded with a smirk. His gaze moved from me to somewhere behind me. I turned around to see Erica. Trying not to over analyze the situation, I just sighed. *Stop being paranoid, Kyrah…*

"I'll see you when I get back Sunday", I said making my way to the driver's side.

"A'ight. See you then." He pecked me on the cheek and walked away. A peck. A damn peck. Not even a kiss. He didn't open the door for me, stop me from walking away, nothing. He was too focused on Erica. I slammed the car door, started the car, and drove out of the parking lot. Something was up and I had to figure what was going on between us.

"Mom, I need to talk to you about something important", I said as my mom and I sat in the kitchen. She was working on her computer and I was nervously contemplating telling her about my mistake with Anthony. But I desperately needed her advice on what I should do.

She looked at me with curious eyes, "I'm listening…"

"Okay… Well, you know Ant and I celebrated four months together, and we just hung out, watched some movies, ate Chinese food and stuff… And…"

"And…?"

"We kinda… I sorta… Ugh… I can't say it. I'm too ashamed." I looked down, hiding my face with my hands. I tried my hardest not to cry again. I was so tired of crying about Anthony.

"Huh—Ohhh… Kyrah…" Tears spilled out of my eyes before I could stop them. I began to sob a little.

"I don't know why I did it. I just know I was so heartbroken after and I couldn't even stand to look at myself. I still can't… And I'm way too ashamed to talk to God. I feel like I've let Him down to the point of no return. And now I have this weird feeling that Anthony's cheating on me with his ex. He's been acting weird and today was the first time we've seen one another all week. He's barely called me. All of our conversations have been under ten minutes. I'm so… I don't know what to do, mommy."

She sighed, "You have to talk to God. He's waiting for you with open arms. I'm disappointed, but I'm glad to see you're taking responsibility for it. And you've learned your lesson. I'm proud of you for being responsible. However, you know what you have to do as far as Anthony goes. You have to do what's right. Go with what you feel in your Spirit. You might have to leave him alone for a while. It doesn't sound like he's good for you spiritually right now."

I sighed as I wiped my face, "You're the second person that's said that."

"Well, God's obviously tryna talk to you. Pay attention."

I nodded, "Thanks, ma." I gave her a hug. "Oh, don't tell dad. I already had a hard time telling you."

She smiled, "Between me, you, and the Lord." I nodded and walked upstairs to my room.

I pulled out my phone as I sat on the bed. My sister wasn't home, so I had the room to myself. I went to my contacts and scrolled until I found Anthony's nickname. I knew what I had to do. Anthony was acting like he wanted nothing to do with me, and I wasn't going to allow him to make a fool out of me.

We need to talk. Call me when you get a chance.

I hit send and waited for him to reply. After five minutes went by, I began to worry. He always texts me back fast. I fought the urge to text him again because I didn't want to seem annoying. After another five minutes passed, I decided to distract myself. Maybe he was just busy. I turned the TV on and chose to watch a comedy on Netflix. That distracted me for a while until I realized how much time had passed: 45 minutes.

An Hour.

Two Hours.

Three Hours.

It was now 8:00 pm and I still hadn't heard from Anthony. I was starting to get pissed. How could he not text me back? I know I sent the message. I'm his girlfriend, although I wasn't entirely confident using that title at this point. I pressed his name on my phone and called him. Voicemail. I threw my phone to the side and shook my head.

"The nerve of this kid…" I said aloud. I ended up waiting another hour until he finally texted me back.

About what? I'm kinda busy.

I scoffed, laughing a bit.

It's cool. Don't worry about it. Handle your business.

After hitting send, my phone almost immediately started ringing. Anthony was calling me. I thought about ignoring him, but I couldn't bring myself to do it.

"Yeah?" I said answering the phone with an attitude.

"Yo, what's your problem? Why you got an attitude?" he asked calmly.

"Excuse me? You're the one that took five damn hours to text me back! Give me one good reason why I shouldn't have an attitude? You have been avoiding me, you didn't open the door for me, you haven't kissed me nor have you held me, you just haven't been paying me any attention since we had sex and I'm really starting to think that you're one of those guys. I saw the way you looked at Erica, too! What we did was a mistake and I'm sorry for going along with it. It should have never gone that far! So, yes, I have an attitude! I'm mad! I'm mad at myself! I'm mad at you! You don't get to take the most precious thing I could ever have and treat me like I'm some side ho! I'm supposed to be your girlfriend, Anthony… You haven't treated me like I am ever since we slept together. And now I'm rethinking us altogether."

I had never felt so relieved. I needed to get that off of my chest. I just hate I had to do it over the phone.

"Kyrah, I tried to be there. That night! I tried. You steady always pushin' me away! Stop blaming me for all your guilt because you didn't even try to talk to me!"

"You didn't try hard enough! Anthony, you knew how much saving myself meant to me… And I'm not blaming you for anything. I had just as much to do with it as you did. But come on, I just needed you to try to understand. But instead, you blow me off for a whole week, and make googley eyes at your ex!"

"Why do you keep bringing Erica up, man?" he asked in an exhausted tone. I could tell he was tired of me mentioning her, but I didn't care.

"Because I just… I don't know… She just keeps popping up! What am I supposed to think, Anthony?"

He paused for a moment before responding, "Look, I'on wanna argue wit' you. Can we finish this when both of us have cooled down? Maybe when you come back tomorrow? I don't wanna go to bed pissed off at you."

I sighed, "I guess you're right. Sorry for having an attitude."

"Stop apologizing. You good, ma. I'll see you tomorrow. I love you, a'ight? Don't think otherwise. I really do love you."

I rolled my eyes. Part of me just wanted to slap him, but the other side of me wanted to give him the benefit of the doubt. "Alright… I love you, too." I pressed "End" and placed my phone down beside me. I let out a groan of frustration. I was beyond exhausted, mentally, anyway. Anthony was just all around a headache. I did love him, but he keeps showing why falling for him was a mistake. Sleeping with him was an even bigger one. What was I supposed to do? I didn't want to break up with him just yet. I almost felt like I was being too hard on him, but at the same time, it just wasn't any excuse to go so long without making an effort to spend time with your girlfriend. It also wasn't an excuse to give another girl your attention, especially when your girlfriend is standing right in front of you. I plopped on the bed and stared at the ceiling. *Where did we go wrong?*

~~~

As I pulled into the school parking lot, I saw Tamra and Raynah waiting for me at the entrance door. I called them to help me with my stuff because I just didn't want to see Anthony right now. We unloaded my things once I parked my car and made our way to our dorm. After we finally reached our room, we set my things in a secluded corner of my room.

"Thanks, y'all", I said.

"Of course, girl. You know we got you", Raynah said.

I opened my mouth to speak, but we heard a loud knock on the door. We frowned, looking at each other confused.

"Who is that?" Tamra asked. I shrugged and headed towards the door. I looked in the peephole to see Anthony standing there. I rolled my eyes. *What did he want?* Annoyed, I opened the door slowly and looked at him.
~~~

“What, Anthony?” I greeted with an attitude. I was probably being a little harsher than I intended, but he just frustrates me so much.

“Yo, did I do somethin’? Why you ain’t ask me to help you with your stuff?” He asked as he tried to walk past me. I placed my hand on his chest and gently pushed him back outside of the door.

“Yeah, you did. I’m still upset with you, so I didn’t want to see you right now.”

“Look, you need to chill with that attitude—”

“No, you need to get out of my face before I say something I won’t mean.”

He chuckled, getting closer in my face, “So, it’s like that?”

I looked away, “Anthony, please leave me alone. I’m mad at you.”

He grabbed one of my hands and kissed the back of it. “Well, can it wait?”

I gave him a skeptical and confused look. I had no idea what he meant by that. Before I could ask, he smiled that beautiful smile that got me to notice him in the first place.

“Be ready by 7”, he said, still holding my hand.

I shook my head in confusion, “Anthony—”

"You got 6 hours, a'ight?"

Instead of protesting, I just nodded. I couldn't lie, I was sort of excited about what he had planned. He smirked and leaned in to kiss me. It was one of those sweet, tender kisses. I hadn't kissed Anthony like this since we had sex the week before, and I definitely missed it. We parted making me blush. He touched my cheek.

"I love you. I'll see you tonight", he said.

"Okay. I love you, too", I replied. I was in some sort of daze. He nodded and walked away from the door. I let the door close, still trying to bring myself back to reality.

"Hey, Kyrah. Get yo life. Come back to us", Tamra joked.

I looked at her, finally getting myself together. I giggled as she and Raynah laughed at me.

"Sorry… That was just the first time we've kissed since… you know…" I stated.

"Ohhh, yeah", Tamra said catching on.

Raynah frowned and looked at both of us, "Um, excuse me. Did I miss something? What happened?"

I sighed, "Sit down." We all made our way to the couch. I don't know why I so hesitant to tell Raynah since I had already told Tamra. It was still something that made me feel a certain guilt. I took a deep breath before speaking.

“Have you noticed me… maybe glowing a little, lately?” I asked avoiding eye contact with her.

“Hmm…” she paused, “Well, I noticed it Monday, but I figured you changed your skin routine or something. I know you ain’t have sex, so I didn’t really think much of it.”

I looked away so she wouldn’t see my face. I heard her gasp.

“Kyrah… You and Anthony had sex last week?”

Finally looking at her, I nodded. I didn’t smile about it like most people would these days. I was very unhappy about my decision. If I could go back and change it, I would.

“Well, why? How? Did he pressure you? I thought you talked to him! Kyrah, what the hell happened?”

I shrugged, “I don’t know. We were just in the moment. He didn’t pressure me at all. He kept touching me, and I didn’t exactly want him to stop. It just kinda went from there. I don’t know what came over me. I regret it so much. I’ve never felt so guilty and heartbroken about anything before.”

Raynah gave me a sympathetic look as she scooted closer to me. Catching me off guard, she gave me a hug. Raynah's not really an affectionate person like Tamra, so it really surprised me. I smiled and hugged her back. After parting, she still looked at me with sympathy.

"Are you okay, now, though?" she asked concerned.

"Yeah, I'm fine. I just… I don't know. My mom and Tamra both told me that I should be probably just let him go. And I believed them after we first had sex. But I just wanna give him a chance. I don't wanna give up on him, yet."

"Yeah, but you should be careful. Don't give up your goodies anymore. He may be expecting more of that. That's kind of why I don't feel like you should stay with him", Tamra said.

I nodded. She had a point. I gave him what he wanted, and now he's probably expecting me to keep giving it to him. And as much as I wanted Anthony and me to stay together, I just don't think I could keep satisfying his hormones.

~~~

"You look so beautiful", Anthony said as he opened the passenger door for me to get in his car.
~~~

I blushed, “Thank you.” I carefully got in the car and put my seatbelt on. I decided on a cute, knee length dress that fit around my waist, but flowed as it got to the bottom. I set the outfit off with some strappy nude sandal heels, a blue jean jacket, some diamond studs, light makeup, and my big afro.

Anthony hopped in the driver’s side, started the car, and drove out of the campus parking lot. After riding for about ten minutes, I started getting anxious. Tonight, had to be special for Anthony to just tell me to be ready and not tell where we were going.

“Anthony Jamal, where are we going?” I finally asked.

He laughed, “My government name, though?” He continued to laugh for a few more minutes. I just looked at him waiting for him to stop, although I wanted to laugh with him.

“I’m not telling you. It’s a surprise”, he finally answered.

I rolled my eyes, “You know I hate surprises.”

“Yeah, I know… But it’s special. Just give me another fifteen minutes.”

I nodded, “Okay. Fifteen minutes.” He chuckled and kept his eyes ahead.

Fifteen minutes quickly went by, and we finally arrived at a nice-looking cabin resort. I frowned to myself, but quickly fixed my face when Anthony stopped the car. He got out of the driver's side and made his way to help me out of the passenger side. I stepped out of the car while holding his hand. I decided not to ask questions because he probably wasn't going to flat out answer anyway. If anything, he would give me the run-around. He guided me inside the cabin, and we were greeted by an older gentleman that was dressed like a host.

"Good evening, Mr. Wright and Ms. Brown. We are all set for your special evening. If you two would follow me this way", the nice man said as he guided us to a nice deck outside. It was absolutely beautiful. It was candlelit, the night was amazing, and the table setting was so neat. I gasped lightly at the sight. Anthony looked down at me and smiled.

"Here's your table. I will be right back with drinks", the greeter said as we sat down.

"Thank you, sir", Anthony said. The greeter walked away, and I eyed Anthony. "What's on your mind, babe?" he asked.

"What's this about, Anthony? Why'd you do all of this?" I asked genuinely.

He smiled, "You. You just deserve it. I know we've been having a lot of issues lately, but I still want you know how much I care about you. And it may have seemed like I was avoiding you this past week, but that wasn't the case. I was planning this surprise so I could make up for not really caring for you like I should have after we had sex that night. I know it's difficult to put up with me, but I love you, for real. I can't think about not being with you. Ever since I saw you in the vending room and we bumped into each other a few days after that, I knew I had to know you."

I smiled, "Aw, aren't you sweet? I love you, too. I don't want to give up us. I care about you too much to actually stay mad at you. Especially when you do stuff like this."

He chuckled, "Well, I'm glad."

We enjoyed our evening together. Dinner was amazing and we just sat and talked like we hadn't talked in months. I guess not really talking to each other for a week was enough for us. After we ate, we walked around outside and just enjoyed the cool night breeze.

"So, where is this? Is this a cabin or something? Are we staying here?" I asked as we sat on a bench outside cuddled together.

"Yes, yes, and yes", he answered while laughing. "This is our spot for the night, if that's alright with you."

I thought about it. I wasn't exactly sure if this was the smartest thing to do. Of course, spending the night with Anthony would be wonderful but not if it was going to end how it ended the last time we did this. I was afraid of waking up the next day, naked and full of shame.

"Anthony, I don't know", I finally said as I sat up to look at him.

He frowned slightly taken aback. "What? Why? What's the problem?"

"You know what the problem is. I don't want what happened last time to happen again. I—"

"So, what you saying, baby?"

I frowned. How much more specific could I possibly be?

"Us having sex, baby." I paused. "Anthony, that night… I'm having the hardest time forgiving myself. I'm not blaming you at all, because you even asked me if I was sure and I didn't say no. I should have moved away from you when I was thinking about it, but I didn't. I know you mean well, but how can you even expect me to go through that again when you saw how torn I was after we did it?"

"I mean… I at least thought you enjoyed it. I thought maybe you would want to try again. Damn. You really know how to kill the mood."

I shrugged, "Yeah, I guess so…" I looked down at my lap.

"I know you feel disappointed in yourself… But don't you wanna try again?" he asked softly.

I looked at him carefully choosing my words. "Anthony, can I ask you a question?" He looked at me and nodded.

"What happened to you respecting me and my choice to wait?" I anxiously waited for his response. He looked to be in deep thought before he responded.

"I do… I did… I don't know. I just… I wanted you so bad. I still do want you. Do you regret having sex with me, Kyrah?"

I sighed. "Anthony…What happened last week should not have happened at all. And I take full responsibility for my actions—"

"How can you say that? Kyrah, you know how much I love you and I'm personally glad I got to express my love to you." I shook my head becoming frustrated. He just didn't understand and there was no other way I could explain it to him.

"I just… I feel like if you really loved me like you claim you do, you would at least try to understand where I'm coming from… And you wouldn't have ghosted me this week…. But you say it so much, I almost feel like you're trying to convince yourself." I drifted off instant regretting saying that last part.

He looked at me with hurt in his eyes. I looked away.

"Ay, you really feel like that? You don't think I love you?"

I shook my head, "I don't know, Anthony. Sometimes I feel like you do, and other times, I feel like you don't. Like, the way you treated me this past week made me feel like that."

"Baby, look at me", he started as he grabbed a hold of my hand. I looked at him with tears in my eyes. "I love you. I really don't know how else to say it. I know you regret what happened between us, but I can't say I do. I got to show you how much I love you. Why can't you see that? Why won't you let me show you again? Let me prove it to you." He leaned in and kissed me softly. I instantly kissed him back, and when I did, it was magical. "Please, baby", he said in between kisses. He pulled me closer to him as we both got into the kiss.

I knew where this was going, and I knew I should have stopped it. I was at a crossroads. What was I supposed to do? I really wanted him to just understand where I was coming from. But am I the one being selfish? Is it me who's not understanding?

He broke the kiss and looked at me, "Let's try again, baby." He leaned in and kissed away the tears that slipped out of my eyes. Still holding my hand, we stood up. He guided me back into the cabin. We ended up in this beautiful master bedroom that had rose pedals on the floor and dim lit lighting. I sat on the bed knowing what I was about to do. I already felt the guilt. It's not that I didn't want to because physically, I wanted this just as bad. But I wasn't sure if I could bear the guilt again. The fact that I was about to hurt God again, made my heart hurt. Anthony kneeled in front of me and held my face. He gently kissed me. I placed my hands on top of his, which were still holding my face.

Our sweet, innocent kiss eventually turned into a passionate, heated make out. Same routine. Same thing. I ignored the Holy Spirit again. This time, I did it without hesitation. I was going to sleep with this man again. He moved from my lips to my neck like he did the first time. I closed my eyes as I had flashbacks to when we did this before. I began to feel the same bliss. He removed my jacket, moving from my neck to my shoulder. I let out a sigh in response at how good his lips felt against my skin.

“Relax, baby girl”, he said in the abnormal deep voice that I loved oh so much.

He moved back up to my face and looked me in the eyes. All I saw was lust. I needed to back away from all of this now, but once again, my flesh had ahold of me. I couldn’t move away from him because I knew I wanted this as badly as he did. He slowly stood up and removed his shirt. I stared at his body amazed as if I hadn’t seen it already.

He chuckled as he caught me staring, “You ready?” I nodded still looking at him.

He smiled, “I got you. I promise.”

“O-okay…” He climbed over me as I leaned back.

Chapter 12

"Therefore, get rid of all moral filth and the evil that is so prevalent and humbly accept the word planted in you, which can save you." (James 1:21)

I opened my eyes, squinting as the sunlight coming through the big window hit me right in my eyes. I tried to move, but I felt Anthony's arms wrapped tight around me. I tried to move again, but that was a fail. Something was telling me that he secured his grip on me so I wouldn't leave this time. But where was I gonna go? I didn't even know where we were. I sighed, finally giving up.

My thoughts were everywhere. I couldn't lay in his arms and feel the slightest bit of peace. Sex was only enjoyable in the moment, but the after effect was a killer. It's possibly the worst feeling in the world. Although the guilt wasn't as bad as the first time [which worried me], I still didn't feel good about it. I know I let God down once again, and I had been running from Him. I couldn't bring myself to face Him because of what I had done. Now that I had done it twice, I didn't even see how I could face Him ever again.

Interrupting my thoughts, I felt Anthony move. His light snore stopped, and he stretched.

“Hey”, he said in his morning voice. I tried not to be mesmerized by it. It was so similar to his abnormally deep voice, but sexier.

“Hi…” I replied. He removed his arms from around me and stood up.

“You hungry? I can make you some breakfast”, he asked as he slipped a pair of basketball shorts on.

I smiled, “Sure.” He smiled and sat on the bed. He ran his fingers through my curls. I blinked slowly.

“You okay?” he asked sincerely.

I nodded, “Yeah. I’m fine.” He nodded and stood up from the bed. Once he left the room, I sighed. I lied on my back and stared at the ceiling for a few seconds. My phone then rang. I dreaded to answer it. I sat up slowly, holding the bed sheets over me. I checked to see who it was. Tamra. My eyes got big as I realized that I hadn’t let them know where I was. I quickly hit “answer”.

“Hello?”

“Kyrah! Girl! Where are you??? You didn’t come back last night!” she said franticly through the phone.

I sighed, “I’m still with Anthony. I’m okay.”

I heard her sigh in relief, “Oh, okay. Well… text me when you’re on the way back.”

“I will, I promise.”

“Okay, bye, girl.”

“Bye.” I pressed the “end” button and placed my phone beside me. I looked down at my body. Still shame. I rolled my eyes getting out of the bed. I decided to take a quick shower so I wouldn’t feel so dirty. The shower helped wash the physical shame, but I still felt nasty inside. I was feeling empty, like I was losing myself. After I got out of the shower, I washed the tears that managed to escape off my face and brushed my teeth. I took the stretched headband off my wrist and put my hair in a puff. I found an extra pair of basketball shorts and a t-shirt that Anthony had and put them on. I grabbed my phone, left the room and met Anthony in the kitchen.

He turned around and looked at me. He smiled.

“I’m almost done”, he said turning back around to finish cooking.

I smiled, “Take your time. I’m not rushing you.” I sat on one of the stools behind the kitchen island. He winked at me making me blush.

He finally finished cooking and he fixed me a plate. He gave it to me, and I quickly dug in. I was super hungry.

"So… Talk to me. What's on your mind?" Anthony asked as he sat beside me with his plate of food.

I swallowed the food I had in my mouth and looked at him. "What are you talking about?"

He shook his head, "I don't know. You not opening up to me as much anymore. You ain't never this quiet around me. What's going on wit' you?"

I slowly placed my fork on my plate. I was hesitant to answer his question because, honestly, I didn't really have a reason. But I had to be honest, I definitely didn't feel as connected with him.

"I-I honestly don't know. I mean, I don't feel… We're not…" I paused and sighed. I looked at Anthony who was looking at me intently, but sincerely. "Anthony, this feeling of knowing I've slept with you twice is literally killing me on the inside."

He frowned a little, "Baby, I thought you were okay with it?"

"I know, I know... I just felt so guilty after the first time because it's hurt to know that I disappointed God and I didn't save myself for my husband. Anthony, I can't deal with this.

He sighed and shook his head. “Kyrah—”

“I’m hurting on the inside. I thought you could see me. Can’t you see that I’m so heartbroken?”

He stopped eating and pushed his plate away from him. He looked back at me with a serious expression. It almost scared me, but I didn’t show it on my face.

“Look, I get it, but you not gon’ sit here and blame me for your decision. You ain’t have to have sex with me. I asked you both times if you wanted to do this and you said it was fine. Stop tryna have a pity party all the time. You don’t get to make me feel bad for you agreeing to do me. And if I’m not mistaken, you sounded like you had a good time last night and last week, so don’t come at me wit’ all that.”

I looked at him as if he had lost his mind. I was trying to decide whether or not I wanted to go off on him or just walk away. I chose the second option because I just didn’t feel like getting into it with him. It just seemed worthless at this point. Once again, I felt like this was another sign from God telling me to let it go. I didn’t want to, but I knew I had to.

I looked at Anthony and nodded, “Okay.” I got up and walked out of the kitchen, leaving Anthony sitting by himself. I heard him sigh, but I just kept walking. I picked up my phone and called Tamra. She picked up the phone after three rings.

“Hey, Kyrah.” she answered.

“Hey, Tam. Can you come get me? I can text you the address of this place.”

“Whoa, wait. What happened? Where’s Anthony?”

I rolled my eyes, “I’ll explain in the car or when we get back to the school.”

“Okay, I’m on my way. Text me where the place is.”

“Thanks, Tam. I love you. Bye.”

“I love you, too, girl. Bye.” I hung up the phone and looked for a card or something that had the address on it. Finally finding a card for all guests on a dresser, I texted her the address. I was so tired and over dealing with Anthony’s attitude. One minute he was sincere and wanted to respect me; the next minute he was going off on me. I no longer knew how to deal with him or our situation.

Anthony then walked in the room while I was changing into my clothes from the previous night. He stopped by the door, leaned on the door post, and crossed his arms.

“Where are you going? You mad?” he asked with a slight attitude.

I rolled my eyes and kept doing what I was doing. “No. I don’t feel like dealing with this right now.”

“So, whenever your feelings are hurt, you just wanna walk away?”

“No, Anthony! But when my boyfriend comes at me the way you did after answering honestly to a question you wanted to know the answer to, it’s just best I walk away.” I paused for a split second. “You know what? We need a break. I can’t do this right now.”

“Kyrah. Wait.” he said calmly while walking closer to me.

I looked him with anger in my eyes, “No! Get away from me! Don’t touch me. Let me leave. I’m done playing games with you! You don’t get to go off on me because I don’t tell you what you wanna hear! Yes, I had a great time last night. I enjoyed YOU! I enjoyed us being close like that! And yes, it felt good! But that’s just for the moment! You don’t understand how I’m feeling, and you don’t try to! I never blamed you for my decision, but I blame you for not listening and not caring! I’m done, Anthony. I can’t do this anymore.”

By the time I finished yelling at him, I had tears streaming down my face. I began to sob. I couldn’t take any more emotional turmoil. It was slowly killing me spiritually, and I didn’t know what else to do. I was starting to wish I’d listened to Tamra and my mom right after they told me to leave him alone.

I stood there and sobbed as Anthony moved even closer to me. I couldn't even tell him to go away because I couldn't stop crying. He pulled me closer to him and wrapped his arms around me. He kissed the top of my head and rubbed my back to comfort me. I didn't have the energy to fight him off. Crying felt so good, but I was tired of crying. All I did was cry with Anthony. This man had a hold on me, and I needed to end it for good.

My phone vibrated repeatedly, so I assumed it was Tamra. I moved out of Anthony's embrace and answered my phone.

"Hello?" I spoke.

"Hey, Kyrah. Just calling to check on you. What you doing?" my mom responded.

I shook off the shakey voice and put on a fake normal voice. "Nothing, just chilling with Tamra", I lied.

"Oh okay, well, call me later. Love you."

"Okay, mom. Love you too. Bye."

I hung up the phone and sighed. I couldn't wait for Tamra to get here. Being around Anthony was making me angry and I didn't want to feel this way anymore.

"So, you leaving?" he asked me.

I nodded, "It's best for us right now. I need to think."

He hesitated for a minute. He sat on the bed and rested his elbows on his knees.

"Dammit… I keep messing up" he finally said, more to himself.

I said nothing. It was the truth. He kept messing up with me and I knew I had to get away from him before he did worse. I was starting to see just how selfish he was. He could never understand what I was going through emotionally and spiritually. I sat beside him and looked at him.

"I'm sorry", I said almost in a whisper. He looked at me as a tear slipped out of his eye. Just the sight of him tearing up made me want to hold him and take back everything I had just said. I loved Anthony, but I felt this relationship going downhill. We needed a break from one another. I didn't want us to stay away forever, but we needed to be apart from one another for a while.

I wiped the tear off his face. My heart was crushed. The last thing I wanted to do was make him cry.

"Shh… don't be. I'm the one that's sorry. I'm losing the best thing that ever happened to me", he replied with a slight frown. I opened my mouth to reply, but my phone began to vibrate in my hand. Tamra's name appeared on the screen and I answered.

"Hey, I'm outside", she said.

"Okay, I'm coming." I hit the "end" button and stood up. I knelt in front of Anthony and grabbed his hands.

"You're not losing me. We both just need times to ourselves. I still love you, but I have to remove myself from this situation for a while before I lose myself. I don't want to, but I need to", I said looking him straight in his eyes.

His face softened as more tears rolled down his cheeks. "I understand, baby girl. Do what you have to do. We can still be friends, right?"

I smiled as my eyes watered, "Of course." I leaned in to kiss him for the last time for a while. "I'll see you around." I grabbed my shoes, jacket, and purse and left him sitting on the bed. I quickly walked out of the cabin and got into Tamra's car.

"Hey," she greeted.

I looked at her, "Hey. Thanks for coming to get me."

"Girl, it's nothing. You okay, though?"

I shook my head, "No… But I will be.

It's been a few days since Anthony and I went on break. Part of me just wanted to accept this as a full-on breakup, but the other part of me was still holding on to the fact that we could get back together eventually. I was even starting to feel bad for breaking up with him in the first place, but I knew it was for the best. The direction we were going in was causing our relationship to become toxic. While Anthony was used to having sex, I just couldn't stomach the guilt and the shame.

Trying to remove the thoughts of Anthony out of my head, I decided to go for a run. A run was just what I needed to clear my thoughts. I don't know how long I ran. The campus was a pretty decent size, so I ran along the sidewalk by the dorms. I ran, and ran, and ran until I felt someone bump into me. Me being the clumsy person I am, I fell on my butt.

"Ow…" I said more to myself.

"My fault! Here, let me help you up," the voice said.

I took the person up on their offer and grabbed their hand. They pulled me off the ground and I dusted myself off.

"Yo, I'm sorry. I should've been paying attention," the person said.

Recognizing the voice, I looked up. *Oh, I know this guy. I can't remember his name, though? John? No. Jake? No. Jimmy? Ugh!*

"It's okay, really. It was my fault, also," I responded. I couldn't remember his name, but I was hoping he would recognize me.

"Hey, I know you. We danced together at that crazy party. Jesse, remember?"

Yes! "I definitely remember you. It's nice to see you again," I replied with a smile. *He is way cuter than I remember...*

"Yeah, you too. Hopefully we'll bump into each other again." He laughed, "See you around."

"See you." I watched him run off and I continued my run. I didn't run for much longer after that. I decided since it was starting to get a little dark outside, I would go back to my room and shower.

On the way back to my building, I walked past Anthony and Erica and a few other people. Erica was sitting on his lap playing with his hair and he had one of his arms around her waist. He wasn't really paying attention to her because he was talking to one of his friends. *What was he doing with her?* Erica saw me passing and smiled and waved at me maliciously. Anthony followed her gaze and stopped once he saw me. I quickly looked away and proceeded to where I was going. As I was waiting for the elevator, Anthony ran to my side.

"Kyrah! Wait," he said making his way to me.

I looked at him puzzled. Why he was talking to me was beyond me. I waited for him to continue.

"Hey… What you saw out there… It wasn't what it looked like", he explained.

I frowned, "Anthony, you don't owe me an explanation. We're not together. Go, do you." The elevator arrived and I got on. Anthony and I made eye contact as the elevator doors closed. I sighed and kept in the tears that I felt coming. I couldn't do anything about the situation, because like I said, we weren't together anymore, so what was there to worry about? I will admit, it's hard to see him with someone else, especially Erica.

I walked back in my room and saw Tamra and Raynah sitting in the living room with two guys I'd never seen before and Raynah's boyfriend, Tommy.

"Oh, snap! Y'all got another roommate?" one of the guys asked.

"Duh. What the hell did you think we had another room for?" Raynah asked.

"Look, ma…" was all I heard after that. I zoned them out and looked at Tamra. I gave her a look as if to tell her to come to my room so we can talk. She nodded and stood up.

"I'll be back," she told one of her friends. She followed me to my room, and I left the door cracked.

"What's up, girl?" she asked. I began pacing back and forth. I wanted to make sure what I was about to say wasn't going to sound stupid or pitiful. Although I was a little hurt by what Anthony said back at the cabin, he was right. I had to stop having pity parties all the time.

"I… I just saw Anthony outside with some friends and that chick Erica was sitting on his lap and was playing in his hair and…" I paused. "It just kinda rubbed me the wrong way. I didn't even do anything. I just kept walking. He tried to explain it to me, but I told him it wasn't necessary. But I don't know… And I know we're not together right now, but… It's only been a few days and I'm trying to shake it off, but I can't. What the hell is wrong with me?" I stopped pacing and plopped on my bed.

She sat beside me, "Girl, calm down! Stop cussing. It's weird… Look, it's perfectly normal to be jealous, but you have to remember why you let him go in the first place. This jealousy won't last forever. Let him do what he wants to do anyway. It's okay. Stop making a big deal about it. You did the right thing by not acknowledging him when you saw him."

I nodded. She was right. Then again, Tamra seemed to always be right when it came to my issues. I looked at her and sighed.

"I'll do the best I can."

She laughed, "I'll take that." I laughed with her.

"Okay, go back to your guest. I'm gonna do some homework."

She nodded, "Alright. Come hang out when you finish."

I nodded and she left the room. I didn't have much homework to do so I finished it pretty quickly. I figured I could take a quick shower then go hang with Tamra and Raynah for a little while. After getting out the shower, I quickly put on some clothes and sprayed some perfume on. I walked into the living room to find everyone watching a movie and eating pizza.

"Finally! Sit, sit! We're just about to watch a movie. Grab some pizza, too," Raynah said making room for me on the couch to sit down. I happily grabbed two slices of pizza and sat beside her. There was a knock on the door, and we all turned our attention to it. They all looked at me like I was supposed to answer it.

"What? Why do I have to get it?" I asked confused.

"Because you the last one that sat down," one of those boys said.

I rolled my eyes, “Fine.” I got up and walked towards the door. Without checking the peephole, I swung the door open to find, Jesse? He looked up from his phone and stared at me. He smiled.

“I’m sorry, do I have the wrong room? Anyone named Tamra stay here?” he asked politely.

“Oh! Yeah, you’re in the right place. Sorry! Come on in,” I greeted him and moved out of the way. He walked in and followed me to the couch. He spoke to everybody and sat beside me. I couldn’t help but feel awkwardly nervous. The whole time we were watching the movie, I ignored Jesse. I ignored everyone, actually. I did nothing but stare at the TV because I couldn’t get my mind off Anthony and Erica. It was hard to shake the image out of my head, but I had to realize that we were no longer together and that he could do whatever he wanted to.

Chapter 13

"Therefore do not let sin reign in your mortal body so that you obey its evil desires." (Romans 6:12)

Almost a month has gone by since Anthony and I broke up and admittedly, every day was getting somewhat easier. I started going back to Bible Studies, but I still felt disconnected from God. My relationship with God hasn't been the same since I first slept with Anthony. I still couldn't bring myself to talk to Him about what I had done. I know He loves me anyway, but I couldn't feel it. I was feeling empty inside. I've prayed, and I knew He was listening, but I felt sorrow because of what I had done to Him. I knew I needed to talk to Him, I just couldn't figure out how to. I know God still cared about me. I'd grown closer with Tam and Raynah and some of their friends which was exactly what I needed at this time. We had all become one big bunch. Being around them helped me get my mind off of Anthony. It was hard to think that he and I were potentially done for good, but maybe it just wasn't meant to be.

I was sitting at a table by myself in the cafeteria doing some homework and listening to music. While I was in the middle of writing someone decided to make themselves comfortable at my table. I looked up to see Erica. I rolled my eyes to myself and sighed. Taking my earphones out of my ears, I gave her a fake smile.

"Yes?" I asked politely.

She smiled, "Sitting by your lonesome? Where's your boyfriend? Oh, yeah. I forgot; you don't have one anymore." She chuckled obnoxiously. I clenched my fist trying to restrain myself from choking ~~this bit~~ her.

I just nodded, "So, is that all you wanted to tell me? Don't you have somewhere else to be ignorant at?"

She scoffed, "Listen lil' girl, don't try me—"

"No, you listen. You don't get to prance yourself over here to make fun of me no longer being with Anthony. For starters, I broke things off with him, in more ways than one," I smirked obnoxiously as her eyes got wide.

"And if I'm not mistaken, you two were never exclusive which I'm pretty sure it's the same thing now. So, the next time you wanna come at me like the way you shouldn't have, think before you open your mouth," I continued. She tried to play off her anger and shock with a smirk. She stood up, brushed off her skirt, and walked away. I followed her to see where she was going. I wasn't even surprised when I saw her walk towards Anthony. He looked at me and smirked. I smiled and waved. I didn't even wait for him to wave back. Instead, I just grabbed my books, bag, and cell phone and left the cafeteria.

“Knock, knock”, Raynah said as she softly knocked on my open door. I looked at her, giving her my full attention.

“Girl, your birthday is tomorrow. What are we doing? Let’s go to the club!” she exclaimed.

I laughed and looked at her like she was crazy, “No, ma’am! I will not experience getting drunk and passing out without knowing it again. No thanks.”

She laughed, “I know. I’m joking. But seriously, what do you want to do? It’s your birthday. We gotta do something. You’re turning nineteen.”

I frowned, “What’s so special about nineteen? Besides, I don’t even know what there is to do here besides eat. Y’all wanna eat? That’s all I can think of.”

She smiled, “Whatever you want, Cupcake. We’ll go eat. Think about where you wanna go and get back at me.”

I nodded and she left my room. I wasn’t particularly excited about my birthday. Although I was starting to get over my breakup, I was still a little sad that I wouldn’t be celebrating with Anthony. After my little episode with Erica, I wasn’t even sure if it was okay for me to miss him like this. Should I miss him at all? I know it's normal, but knowing him, he was probably messing around with Erica again. And one thing's for sure, I wasn't going to be with him if he was still sleeping with her. In my mind, this "break" had become a real breakup. I mean, I told him we could be friends, but he's been so in Erica's face, he hasn't made an effort to be my friend. I took that as us being friends not being good enough for him, so I let it go.

Removing myself from my thoughts, I put my workout clothes on. I needed to go for a run so I could stop thinking so much. Thinking wore me out, so I figured a good run would help me. After I got dressed, I grabbed my phone, earphones, and room key. Before I left, I called Jesse to see if he wanted to run with me. After he agreed, he said he would meet me downstairs. I quickly left my room and made my way downstairs so I wouldn't keep him waiting. I ended up waiting for him for five minutes, but once he came down, we took off.

"You must be bored since you hit ya boy up", he joked.

I rolled my eyes, "Shut up. You're my friend. Don't play."

He laughed, "I know." We ran for a few miles before we started walking for a while.

"I needed to clear my mind. Running helps me stop overthinking. Talking to someone helps me stop thinking period," I admitted as we were walking slowly.

He looked at me and nodded. "Me too. I'm glad you called me, though."

"Yeah? Why's that?"

He smirked, "One, I enjoy being around you and I wanted to see you, anyway." A small smile formed on my lips. "And two, I was ordered to help you figure out what the hell you wanna do for your birthday."

My smile quickly disappeared as he finished his statement. I rolled my eyes.

"I'm gonna kill Raynah." He laughed.

"I told her I wanted to go eat somewhere. I just don't know where," I finished.

He shrugged, "What do you have a taste for?"

"I don't know. I'll figure it out. I don't wanna think about that right now." He nodded in understanding. We continued our run for another fifteen minutes before we decided to call it quits. As we were walking towards our building while talking, I saw Anthony and his same crew in the same place I saw them last time I went running. He gave me an intense look before getting up to walk towards us. I stopped Jesse from walking and turned towards Anthony.

“Hey,” he greeted. He gave Jesse a rude look but gave him a head nod.

“Hi,” I responded.

“Who this?” he asked.

I frowned, “Um, my friend, Jesse. You remember him from the party?”

He nodded, “Oh, yeah. I remember when you danced with my girl.”

Jesse frowned then looked at me, “Aye, I’ma head up to my room. I’ll hit you up later. Let me know when you get in your room.”

I nodded, “Okay. Bye, Jesse.” I gave Anthony an annoyed look.

“What the—what was that? We’re not together anymore, Anthony!”

He looked at me and shrugged. A smirk formed on his face, “How can you be friends with that clown?”

“The only clown I see is the one standing in front of me talking reckless. Go back to your friends and leave me alone, please.” I turned around and walked inside the building. After getting my card swiped, I hurried to my room. I shot Jesse a quick text and made myself comfortable on the couch. I had way too much to think about. Unfortunately, that run did nothing but make everything worse. Maybe I should've gone alone. Or maybe I should've just ignored Anthony and carried on to my room.

I sighed and closed my eyes. I quickly opened them, jumping as Tamra and Raynah burst in the door. Tamra looked at me and laughed.

"Girl, our bad! We ain't mean to scare you," she apologized.

I chuckled, "It's fine. I'm gonna go shower then we can talk about tomorrow."

They nodded in response. I hurried into the shower. I tried to clear my mind there, but nothing could put my mind at ease right now. After that encounter with Anthony, I just wanted to go to sleep. He has a way of getting under my skin, and now that we're not together, it's more annoying than anything. I loved him, of course, but he was starting to become less desirable. I see the way he is around Erica and the way she is with him. It's obvious that I was nothing more than a notch on his belt. I don't care what he says, what they had was something serious, especially for him to go right back to her after he and I broke up… Like, literally right after we broke up.

I shook my head and got out of the shower. My mind wandered everywhere at this point. I found myself wondering what he was doing, what he saw in Erica. *I mean, she's a very pretty girl. She's beautiful, actually, but she's so stuck up and rude. I could never understand why he's attracted to that.* I rolled my eyes at my thoughts. I was tired of thinking about him and our non-situation. Finally finishing my after-shower routine and putting on a pair of shorts and a tank top, I walked back into the living room area and sat on the couch with Tamra and Raynah.

"Alright, birthday girl. You gotta tell us what you wanna do before I drag you to a club. And this time I'm serious," Raynah said.

I laughed, "Okay! Okay… Let's go get some Hibachi. I'm craving some sushi."

Tamra nodded, "Sounds good. Let's do it. By the way, I will be paying for your meal, so you don't have to worry about money or anything. I will not take "no" for an answer because it's settled, 'kay? 'Kay." I rolled my eyes to myself. I hated when people paid for things for me because I always feel like a burden. Instead of arguing with her, I just nodded and smiled.

We relaxed for a while before deciding to all go to bed. Tomorrow was something that I was slowly starting to look forward to. Although I was a little disappointed, I figured that I couldn't do anything about it and decided to brush it off. Tomorrow was going to be a good day, and I couldn't let anyone ruin it.

Chapter 14

"Above all, love each other deeply, because love covers over a multitude of sins." (1 Peter 4:8)

I woke up to the sun shining in my face through my window. I smiled as I stretched. Today was a beautiful day to turn nineteen and I was excited. I got out of my bed and walked out of my room to find Tamra already awake washing her face. She looked at me through the mirror, stopped what she was doing and smiled widely. She ran to me and hugged me.

"HAPPY BIRTHDAY TO ONE OF MY FAVORITE PEOPLE!" she exclaimed in my ear.

I laughed, "Thank you, lil' shawty!" She let go of me still smiling.

"You excited for today? I can't wait. I might be a little more excited than you."

I smiled. "You might just be", I joked. "But no, I am excited for today. Nothing is going to ruin this day. I'm excited to be spending it with you guys."

"Good for you, girl", she replied smiling. She went back to do what she was doing, and I went back in my room. I decided to leave the door open. As I sat on my bed, my phone began to ring. I frowned when I saw who it was because I wasn't expecting them to call. *Anthony?* Seeing his name appear on my screen reminded me that I had to remove all those emojis from his name and actually change his name to "Anthony". After a few more seconds, I finally answered.

"Hello?"

"Hey! Happy birthday. I just wanted to call and let you know I didn't forget about you" he said in what sounded like his morning voice. *Oh, how I miss his voice.*

I smiled to myself, "Well, thank you. I really appreciate you calling me."

"Of course. Anything for you, baby girl." My heart began to beat fast and I was suddenly feeling sad. I couldn't lie, as much as I wanted to choke him yesterday, I missed him so much. Being called "baby girl" didn't make it any better either.

"So, you got any plans for today?" he asked breaking the silence.

I cleared my throat getting myself back together, "Yeah. I'm hanging out with the girls later. Gonna go get some dinner. I don't know what else they have planned, though."

He chuckled, “Cool. Sounds fun. Well, enjoy your day.”

“Thank you, I will.”

“Hey… I miss you.” I exhaled deeply in response because I felt myself getting sad again. The last thing I needed was to be moping around because I missed my ex-boyfriend and we weren’t together for my birthday. As tempting as it was for me to get all mushy with him and run to his room and lie in his arms, I knew I couldn’t.

“Ditto,” I responded with a giggle.

He chuckled lightly, “A’ight. I’ll talk to you later.”

“Okay. Bye.” I slowly removed the phone from my ear and pressed “end” on the screen. Tamra then walked in my room and placed her hands on her hips. I looked at her and sighed. *She’s so nosy.*

We looked at one another for a while before she laughed.

“Girl, you got it bad. You miss that boy.”

I smiled. She was right. I was almost starting to feel like our breakup was a big mistake. Although I knew it was what I needed to do, I had been secretly hoping this wasn’t a forever thing. I would have days like yesterday when I was glad I was done with him. I just hated that I was starting to miss him even more on the day that I was hoping would completely distract my mind from him.

"You look so fine! You gotta stop tryna make me like you like that, girl! I like boys, darn it" Tamra exclaimed as we were all walking out of the main door of our room.

"I know right? Gon' mess around and have another boyfriend by the end of the night. Better quit teasing these boys on this campus," Raynah agreed.

I laughed, "I swear, you guys are extra. I'm not trying to do anything. And please, I'm not tryna date anybody else."

I was wearing a cute black maxi skirt with long splits on both sides and a blue crop top. I put on some cute blue strappy blue sandals to match set off the outfit. Raynah straightened my hair for me, and I accessorized it with big silver hoops, and a black necklace. I even did a full face for my makeup because I felt it was appropriate. I felt really pretty and was ready for people to see me. Raynah even had the bright idea to buy me a birthday tiara so everyone would know it was my birthday.

We finally made our way downstairs into the lobby to meet Jesse and his friend, Sean.

“Birthday girl! You look beautiful” Sean said as he gave me a hug. I smiled as I hugged him back. “Happy birthday”, he finished.

“Thank you, Seany!” I said as we parted from one another.

I hugged Jesse, and he hugged me a little bit longer.

“Happy birthday, baby,” he said in my ear.

“Thank you.” He smiled as we parted. I had been feeling Jesse for a while now, but I just pushed the feelings aside. We all stood in lobby and conversed for a little while. Jesse kept staring at me making me blush, but I just brushed it off. I was starting to like him a lot, but I wasn’t sure if I was ready to be with someone else. While I was talking to Tamra and Sean, the door of the main entrance opened. I looked to see who it was: of course, it was Anthony. And he was with Erica. *But you miss me, though? Yeah, right.*

He didn’t see me at first, probably because he didn’t recognize me with my hair straight. He finally looked at me and stopped paying attention to Erica. A smile grew on his face and I smiled back. I turned my attention back to Tamra and Sean so I wouldn’t keep staring at him.

“Okay, guys. I made reservations for 7:30. It’s 6:50. We need to get up out, so let’s go”, Raynah said over everybody. We all nodded and proceeded out of the door. As I was walking out, I felt a hand gently grab my free hand. I turned around to find Anthony. I smiled politely.

"I didn't even recognize you. You look beautiful", he said.

"Thanks. I decided to do something different."

Tamra then came back in the door and grabbed my hand, "Girl, come on."

I laughed, "Okay, give me a sec." She looked at Anthony then back at me and nodded. She walked back out of the door. I turned my attention to Anthony who was staring at me in admiration.

"Well, I don't want you to get left. Have fun. You look amazing" he said while grinning.

I smiled, "Thank you, Anthony. I appreciate it." He leaned down and kissed me on the cheek. I blushed and left him standing there. I tried the best I could to remove him from my brain so I wouldn't spend the rest of the night thinking about him. I met Tamra outside and we walked to her car. We all left and headed to the restaurant.

The ride to the restaurant was fairly long which was why Raynah was in such a rush. I was excited to be spending my birthday with them. We listened to every trap song [which is a lot] I had on my phone and danced and rapped all the words. Having fun in the car was my way of distracting myself from my thoughts about Anthony. Hearing his voice and then seeing him made me miss him even more. I couldn't front like him taking the time to wish me a happy birthday didn't warm my heart, especially after how I talked to him yesterday. I just wish he would stop popping up everywhere.

We arrived at the restaurant after a twenty-minute ride. We made it with five minutes to spare, thank God.

"Hello, how many?" the hostess asked with a genuine smile.

"We have a party of 8 under Thomas for 7:30", Raynah responded.

The host checked the list then looked back at us and smiled, "Just in time. Follow me." She grabbed menus and led us to our hibachi table. We found our seats, and of course, I sat in the seat that was decorated with balloons. Right after the hostess left, our waiter came and took our orders.

"Kyrah, you look real good tonight, baby," Jesse said in his thick Atlanta accent.

I smiled and blushed, "Thanks." I winked at him and blew him a kiss. Jesse and I genuinely flirted from time to time. I thought he was extremely cute, but he knew I wasn't ready to be with anybody else.

He smirked, "Girl, you better stop before I give you the best birthday present of your life. I'll take you back to the school so fast and-"

"Jesse!" Tamra exclaimed. We all laughed at his comment. I knew he was joking, but him saying that really made me think of Anthony. Maybe that's why I thought Jesse was so cute. He reminded me a lot of Anthony, although I was so sure no one could ever amount to the first guy I've ever loved. I caught myself staring at Jesse with a sense of lust. I was somewhat mesmerized by his beautiful, long locs and his full lips, and his beautiful caramel skin. Half of his locs were up in a messy bun, and the rest hung neatly down his back showing off his gorgeous face. He sort of resembled Quavo from Migos, but only a little. He looked up and caught me looking at him. He smirked and I blushed. *What is up with me and these guys with locs? Get it together, girl. Chill with the lusting.*

I quickly looked away from Jesse and distracted myself with the conversation that was taking place between Sean and Tamra. The rest of the dinner went smoothly. We ate, laughed, joked, and just had a good time. Raynah had to leave early to go pick her boyfriend up from work. I was a little disappointed, but I knew she would've stayed if she could have.

Although Jesse and I kept making eye contact during our time there, I managed to keep myself together. *Lord, help me.* I somewhat knew that little silent prayer I said wasn't going to help. I rolled my eyes to myself. We left the restaurant and headed back to our dorm.

"Kyrah, what's up with you?" Tamra asked randomly while we were riding in the car. She and I were in the back seat of her car while Sean and another one of the boys, CJ rode in the front seat.

I looked at her and frowned, "What? Nothing! Why?"

"You seem a little… different. Not in a bad way, but… I don't know. You okay?"

I'm feeling something… I just need Jesus to keep me away from Jesse.

Pushing my thoughts out of my head, I nodded. "Yeah, I'm cool."

She nodded, leaving the subject alone. The rest of the ride back to the school went by pretty fast. We all got out of the cars and headed in our building. After checking in at the front desk, we all headed to our room.

"Hey, can you open the door for me? I lost my card somewhere in my purse", Tamra said as she searched her big purse.

I chuckled, "Okay." I pulled my key out and opened the door.

"SURPRISE!" People yelled as I opened the door. I jumped and held my chest. Tears began to fill my eyes as I covered my mouth.

"I hate y'all," I said as a few tears slipped. I put my fist up when I spotted Raynah and she laughed. Everyone laughed as I walked in. Everyone that was there wished me a happy birthday as I passed them. I didn't know everybody there, but I was glad to see people come celebrate my day with me. I looked around to see if Anthony would show up, but I knew that was a loss cause. Why would he come to my party? He was probably laid up with Erica, anyway. I sighed and spotted a seat on the couch. Everyone was sitting around, or dancing to the music that played loudly. I was laughing at some people as I observed by myself. Jesse walked in my direction and sat beside me.

"Why you sittin' down? This yo' party!" he said with a playful frown.

I laughed, "I know that, sir. My feet hurt and I just like observing."

He smirked and grabbed my hand. "Lemme holla atchu' real quick." I nodded and stood up. I followed him to my room. He closed the door and grabbed my waist. I giggled in response. *Why am I giggling? No, this is not okay! Run, Kyrah! Run!* He smiled his million-dollar smile.

"Why you was lookin' at me like that at dinner?" he asked.

I rolled my eyes playfully, "Does it matter why? You liked it."

He chuckled lightly, "You right. I did. I mean, though… Wassup?" *Whew, Lord. I shouldn't even be in here with you, but I can't move.*

"I should be asking you that." I replied in a teasing tone. *That wasn't supposed to come out…*

He smirked, pulling me closer to him. He leaned down and kissed me softly. I kissed him back, wrapping my arms around his neck. I knew what was about to happen. I knew I had to stop it. But the question is, did I want to?

We kissed for a while. I played in his locs as he ran his hands up and down my back. He wasn't as gentle as Anthony, but I didn't mind. I actually liked it. It helped me keep my mind off of him. He locked the door, still kissing me, and we moved to the bed. He gently pushed me on the bed and took his shirt off. I bit my lip as I looked at the tattoos on his chest. He smiled and climbed on top of me. *Are we really going to do this with all these people here? But what if he stops liking me if I don't sleep with him? I shouldn't be doing this... You know what? Forget it.* I felt the Holy Spirit talking to me, but my thoughts and hormones over-talked His voice. I couldn't hear Him clearly.

I became lost in the moment and what was going on. I got lost in Jesse's kisses and his touch. He began kissing me slower, as if to tease me, so I went along with it. He kissed me on my neck for a while, almost as if he were trying to give me a hickey. I giggled a little at the feeling. He moved back to my lips. I broke the kiss and looked at him.

"You have condoms?" I asked. I cursed myself in my head. *Why did I ask that? Now I've definitely gone too far to turn back.*

"Yeah, I gotchu, baby."

I knew I was losing myself. How did I go from not wanting to be near sex, to sleeping with another guy? I knew this was wrong, and I knew I should've stopped. But I just couldn't.

We lied in my bed and stared at the ceiling. I looked at him and caught him staring at me.

"What?" I asked, blushing.

"You know I like you, right?"

I smiled, "I know. I like you, too..."

He nodded, “Cool. I know you not tryna be wit’ anybody right now after ya homeboy, and I’on wanna rush you or nothin’… But, would you date me if I asked you, maybe in the future?”

I thought about his question. I wouldn’t mind dating him, but I was afraid that I would treat him as a rebound. Plus, what we just did was not okay. Why couldn’t he just confess his feelings before? Whatever. I couldn’t risk a heartbreak again, but I didn’t want to turn him down because I really did like him.

He stared at me waiting for my answer. I took a deep breath and looked back at him.

“Maybe…”

He smiled, “I’ll take that.” He leaned over and kissed me sweetly on the lips. We were interrupted by a knock on the door.

“Kyrah! You in there?” I heard Raynah’s voice from the other side. We both quickly got out of the bed and hurried to put our clothes back on.

“Yeah, I’m in here! I’ll be out in a sec!”

“Okay! We’re about to pull the cake out. Everything ok??”

“Yeah, I’m fine. I just needed to get away for a few minutes! I’ll be right out.”

"Okay, hurry!" I finished adjusting my clothes, carefully checking myself in the mirror. I decided to leave my shoes off, since my feet were hurting anyway. I looked at Jesse and helped him adjust his clothes.

"Okay, you hurry into the bathroom as I go into the living room. Flush the toilet so it'll seem realistic," I said.

He nodded, "Bet. Let's do this." I carefully opened the door so I wouldn't attract attention. Jesse snuck in the bathroom with ease, so I walked into the living room.

"There you are!" Tamra exclaimed as she pulled me towards the beautiful birthday cake, they got me. I smiled and stood in front of it.

"Where's Jesse?" Raynah asked. I heard the toilet flush and he walked out the bathroom not too long after. After washing his hands, he made his way into the living room and stood with everyone else. Tamra lit the candles and everyone sang "Happy Birthday" to me. I blew out the candles and everyone cheered. Tamra cut up the cake and passed out slices to everyone. After I got my piece, I saw Jesse sitting in a chair by himself. I walked over to him and sat down.

"You okay?"

He looked at me and smiled, "I should be asking you that."

I laughed, "You're annoying." I looked away for a second and spotted Sean looking at us with a smirk on his face. My face burned with blush, so turned my attention back to Jesse.

After about another hour of talking and listening to music, everyone but the usual crew decided it was time to leave. I thanked everyone for coming as they walked out of the door.

"Well, I'ma call it a night," Sean said standing up. CJ soon stood up after Sean.

"Yeah, me, too. I'm tired," he stated while stretching a little bit.

"Well, thanks for celebrating my birthday with me. It means a lot," I said as I walked them to the door. I gave both of them a hug.

"Happy birthday, again, lil' sis," Sean said with a smile.

"Thank you." I smiled. He smiled back and walked out of the room. I closed the door behind them and plopped back on the couch next to Jesse. Raynah smirked and I frowned.

"I think I'm gonna hit the sack. I'll see y'all tomorrow. I hope you had fun, Kyrah, girl!" Tamra said as she hugged me and planted a sloppy kiss on my cheek. I laughed and wiped it off.

"I did! Thank you, guys. I love you guys very much!" Raynah joined the hug and we all laughed. They got off me and headed to their rooms leaving me and Jesse alone. I put my feet in his lap and rested my head on the couch.

"You know… There's plenty more where earlier came from…" he said breaking the silence.

I laughed, "Oh, really? I don't believe you."

"Word? A'ight." He pushed my feet out of his lap and stood up. He picked me up and threw me over his shoulder. I squealed and laughed as he carried me to my room. He closed the door and locked it. *This is going to be a long night…*

Chapter 15

"If we confess our sins, he is faithful and just and will forgive us our sins and purify us from all unrighteousness." (1 John 1:9)

"Kyrah," I heard a soft, deep voice say in my sleep. I thought I was dreaming so I didn't bother opening my eyes. "Kyyyraaahh," the voice sang. I groaned a little. Finally opening my eyes, I woke up to see Jesse in my face. He smiled and I continued to frown.

"Hey," he finally said. I rolled my eyes and put the covers over my face making him laugh.

"Dang, I was just gonna ask if you wanted to go get some breakfast. I know you hungry."

I laughed while still under the covers, "How does one assume that I'm so hungry?"

I waited for him to answer. He then pulled the cover from over my face and climbed on top of me. I laughed again as he kissed me.

"'Cause I put it down, twice." I laughed even harder and pushed him off of me.

I sighed after I finished laughing, "Okay. We can go get some breakfast. I'll meet you downstairs when I get ready."

He nodded, “A’ight. You got thirty minutes.” I giggled and nodded. He got out of the bed and put his clothes on so he could go to his room and get ready. I stood up, still holding the bed covers around me.

“Hurry up,” he joked. I playfully hit him. He leaned down and kissed me and I smiled. He left my room and I closed the door behind him. I quickly hurried to get into the shower so I could get ready to go. It didn’t take me long to shower and put some clothes on. I brushed my teeth and washed my face then touched up my hair. I decided not to bother with any makeup and just put my glasses on. I checked my phone to see that I still had ten minutes to chill.

While sitting on my bed, scrolling on Twitter, Tamra walked out of her room and into mine.

“I thought I heard Jesse in here,” she said making herself comfortable in my lounging chair.

“He was. He left not too long ago.”

She gave me a suspicious look then her eyes got big.

“Kyrah… You didn’t…”

I sighed and nodded, “I know, I know.” I checked my phone to see what time it was. I slowly stood up from the bed and grabbed my purse. I figured I’d better go downstairs so Jesse wouldn’t be waiting for me.

"Where you goin'? We gotta talk!" Tamra fussed as she stood up.

"We'll talk later. I promise. I'll explain everything." She nodded and left my room. I exhaled as I watched her leave. Hurrying out of my room and locking my door, I tried not to think about what she was going to say. I knew what Jesse and I did was wrong, but I was at the point where it didn't matter. Maybe Anthony was right. I did it once, so does it hurt to do it again?

I met Jesse downstairs and we headed out of the building. He drove us to the closest diner and got a table for two. We talked a little while we were waiting for our waiter to come take our drink orders.

"So, what happened with you and ole boy?" he asked randomly.

I sighed, "We just needed a break because things were going left." He looked at me waiting for me to continue. "He was just… He won me over with his charm and he was such a gentleman. He told me that he respected the fact that I wanted to wait to have sex until I was married. He got "saved", supposedly. But then, everything changed. He started throwing hints that he wanted some. I talked to him about it, but we both just got caught up."

"Wait, so last night… Why did you have sex with me?"

"Well… One night, we were in his room watching a movie and we both just kinda fell into a trap. And while I physically enjoyed it, I had a really hard time processing it afterwards. It even felt like he started distancing himself from me after that. But after I confronted him about how he was treating me, he took me to this nice cabin. We had a really nice dinner, then he wanted to do it again. We both did, honestly… But even after expressing how I felt after our first time, he was convinced that we should try again… that maybe it would be different. Even I was convinced, honestly…" I felt the tears welling in my eyes, "I just couldn't understand what was happening to us. We were only together for four months, but I've never cried so much. I love him, still. He was my very first boyfriend. And last night… What he said was true, at least, I think. I already made the mistake, and I can't take it back, so it didn't hurt to try again… I don't know. Plus, I figured maybe you would really want to be with me if I did have sex with you. Get it out of the way already… I didn't realize how much I really liked you until last night."

By the time I finished talking, I had a few tears rolling down my cheeks.

"Don't cry, baby," he said gently as he reached across the table to wipe the tears that had fallen. He held my face and smiled.

"You ain't have to sleep with me. I would've been cool wit'out all'at. Look, you still healin', and I'ma give you time. But I'm not ole boy. I'm sorry he took something that was obviously important to you and then pretty much dissed you. I know you like me but take your time. I'll still be here when you're ready."

I looked at him and smiled. "That's sweet, Jesse."

He smirked, "I ain't gon' lie, though. It was nice. I enjoyed it."

I laughed, "Oh, my gosh…" He laughed with me. Our waiter finally showed up and took our food orders. We ate our food and talked some more. Talking to Jesse was a breath of fresh air. He was right, I was still healing from my breakup with Anthony, but I really wanted to give him a chance. I just wasn't entirely sure if I should.

While we were riding back to the school, he held my hand. It felt nice. I really enjoyed being around Jesse. He brought out a playful side of me that I never knew I had. We shortly arrived back to the school and he put his arm around my shoulder while we walked. On the way inside, we passed Anthony and Erica. Anthony stopped and smirked. I was going to just walk past him until he spoke to me.

"So, you just seeing everybody now? You had to get a knockoff of me, huh?" he asked me.

“Excuse me? I ain’t doin’ nothing you ain’t doin’, sweetheart,” I responded.

He chuckled, “Whatever. You was all on the phone wit’ me yesterday and all in my face and now you in some other dude’s face. That ain’t cute, Kyrah.” I looked at Erica who was looking at Anthony with a frown.

“Aye, bruh. Don’t talk to her like that,” Jesse stepped in.

“And I’on think I was talkin’ to you, dawg” Anthony said walking towards Jesse.

“Man, wassup, bruh. I’m gettin’ real tired of you”, Jesse said walking towards him. I stepped in the middle of them and stopped them from moving any further. I could see the rage in both of their eyes. I looked at Jesse and mouthed for him to relax before turning my attention to Anthony.

“Anthony, if I remember correctly, you called me telling me that you missed me. And it was you that was all in my face yesterday. You remember grabbin’ me and tellin’ me how nice I looked right? And you kissed me on the cheek? Since you wanna act like you got amnesia. Get out my face tryna show out in front of this girl. Stop sweatin’ me so much. You’re not my boyfriend anymore.”

Anthony stood there stunned. I was even shocked I said all that. He nodded and grabbed Erica's hand and walked away. I grabbed Jesse's and we did the same. I was so annoyed by Anthony. I was done with him. *How dare he come in my face questioning me hanging out with somebody else when he's always in Erica's face?* Jesse and I quietly walked to my room. I was completely blowed. I was over Anthony and his wishy-washy attitude towards me. One minute he was in my face saying he missed me and the next minute he wanted to show out for Erica.

As I opened the door, Jesse made sure to stay close to me. I walked straight to my room and he followed. He closed the door behind him and sat on the bed. I slammed my purse, my keys, and my phone down on the desk then plopped on the bed.

Jesse looked at me, "Calm down, baby."

I rolled my eyes, "He always does that! Even when we were dating, he would be cool one minute, then next thing I know, he has an attitude. Then he thinks he can be all with Erica and it's cool, but trip when I'm hanging out with another guy? That's so bewildering! I don't get it, Jesse! I don't understand how men's brains function!" I shook my head, staring straight ahead.

"Kyrah, you need to chill out. Stop letting him get to you. You said it yourself, y'all not dating anymore. Don't let everything he does bother you. And it's obvious he just misses you anyway," Jesse said trying to calm me down.

I looked at Jesse and gave him a small smile. I leaned in and kissed him, softly.

He smirked, "You know, the more you kiss me, I'ma think we together."

I giggled, "Give me some time, okay?"

He nodded, "I gotchu. I ain't goin' nowhere." He kissed me again. "But just so you know, we ain't kissin' no more until we start dating officially. And last night was our last time having sex until we get married. I'm tryna keep you as a good girl."

I frowned and smiled, "Married? You're thinking that far ahead, already?"

He smiled and nodded, "Yep. You gon' be wifey." I laughed, although I knew he was pretty serious. He smiled and looked down at his lap. He looked back at me and stared into my eyes. I blushed. I wanted to look away, but I couldn't. I was captivated by his intense, romantic stare.

"You're so beautiful. So precious. I want to cherish you. You're like… You're like a diamond that has been tossed and turned and treated bad. Like, you shined so bright before you got in the wrong hands. But I wanna help clean you, and polish you, so you'll be good as new. Possibly better. I wanna help you getcha shine back."

I stared back at him, my mouth slightly opened. I was in awe. *Where did that come from?*

"Jesse… I-I—"

He grabbed my hand, "You don't have to respond. I just want you to know that I gotchu. A'ight?"

I nodded and bit my bottom lip slightly. I smiled.

"That was really sweet, Jesse."

"That's all I'm tryna be to you," he replied with his gorgeous smile. For the first time in the last few months, I was able to see myself with someone other than Anthony. I could look at someone and see something far more beautiful than Anthony. Never did I think, especially not these last few months, anyone would amount to Anthony. I felt all my feelings, love, hate, sorrow, for him begin to fade.

I leaned over and hugged Jesse. He exhaled and wrapped his arms tight around me. I smiled to myself.

"I can't wait," I said aloud.

"Me neither, baby."

It's been two days since Jesse poured out his heart to me and we've been talking almost nonstop since then. We talked about everything. I really felt like I could easily talk to him without feeling like he just wanted me for something other than myself. Although I never really made it known that I felt that way with Anthony, I always knew he didn't really love me. Or maybe he did, he just went about it the wrong way.

I was walking from class on the way to the cafeteria when I passed Erica. I decided today would be a good day to practice being nice.

"Hi, Erica," I said with a genuine smile this time.

She looked at me, obviously shocked. "Um… Hi…? What do you want?"

I shrugged, "I was just speaking. Have a nice day." I smiled once more and began to walk away until she stopped me.

"Kyrah, wait…" I stopped and turned to see what she wanted.

"Yeah?"

She sighed. "I don't know what you have… Had with Anthony, but it was obviously really special. I'm very envious of that. Even when he's with me, you come around and he forgets I'm there. You're obviously a beautiful girl, and you seem nice. Maybe that's why he loves you so much. You deserve him." She looked down and wiped her face of the few tears that managed the slip.

I frowned. I felt sorry for her. I don't know where all that came from.

"Erica… You're a very beautiful girl. And even if Anthony makes you feel otherwise, it's the truth. You honestly deserve someone better. Anthony… He and I just aren't for one another. But you shouldn't let him walk all over you. End it before it goes too far."

She looked at me and smiled, "Thanks. That was really nice of you to say…"

I returned the smiled, "No problem." We stood there for a moment. I debated on if I wanted to invite her to eat lunch with me or not. Before I could really think about, the words slipped out of my mouth.

"You wanna eat lunch with me? I would really like for us to really get past this beef."

She nodded, "Sure. I would like that." We walked into the cafeteria together and found a spot to sit. After getting our food, we sat and talked. I found that Erica was a very sweet girl. She had a nice personality, along with her great looks. We chatted for a while until we decided it was time to go. As we were leaving, we approached Anthony and some of his friends. He stopped walking and frowned.

"Hey, Erica," he greeted her, completely ignoring the fact that I was standing there. I raised an eyebrow, debating on if I should say something, but I decided against it.

I touched Erica's arm and smiled, "See you around."

She smiled, "Okay. See ya." I looked at Anthony and rolled my eyes. I walked past him and proceeded out of the cafeteria. On the way out, I saw Sean walking in my direction. Once he saw me, he greeted me with a big smile.

"Wassup, Kyrah," he stated as he gave me a quick hug. I tried my hardest to match his energy and give him a genuine smile, but I couldn't. I was highly annoyed with Anthony's attitude towards me and just couldn't shake it.

"Hey, Sean," I finally responded. He looked at me, searching my face. A slight frown etched his forehead.

"You look like you need to talk so let's go take care of that."

I couldn't even argue with his statement because deep down I knew he was right. I followed him to the nearest shaded bench that sat right in front of the Intramural field. We sat in silence for a few moments.

Gathering my thoughts seemed like an impossible task at the moment. Sean let out a deep sigh and leaned forward, resting his elbows on his legs.

"So, what's goin' on? You seem like you got a lot on your mind," he said breaking the silence. I took a deep breath and shrugged.

"I'm… I feel like so much is happening to me right now. I have these sudden feelings for Jesse, but I'm a little hesitant about them because I just got out of a relationship. And speaking of that, my ex acts like he hates me. He said he wanted us to still be cool, but he's done nothing but act like a complete jerk towards me. My emotions are just all over the place right now. I don't know what to do about any of it." I looked at Sean who looked as if he was choosing his next words carefully. He nodded a little before speaking.

"A'ight, as far as your ex goes, I'm not excusing the way he's been treating you. That's not cool at all… but he's honestly probably more upset at himself for losing you and he just doesn't know how to deal with that. It's not right, but I think you just gotta forgive him and move on. He'll come around eventually."

I nodded as I listened carefully to everything he was saying. He was right, but I still couldn't shake the different emotions I was feeling. If Anthony loved me the way he said, why did he treat me so horribly? I only broke up with him because I didn't want our relationship to ruin us both.

"And as far as Jesse…" he started, "I already knew about y'all having something goin' on." He chuckled and I joined him. His face then became a little serious as he looked at me sincerely.

"But I'ma tell you this as a friend and as someone who doesn't want to see you get your heart broken. Jesse's my boy, but I just want you to be careful. He's got some history and like you said, you just got out of a relationship. I'd hate for you to get hurt all over again. And I don't wanna have to beat nobody up."

Deep down, I wanted to take heed to his warning, but I also wanted to give Jesse a chance. A sigh fell from my lips and I nodded. Sean nudged me gently.

"Just be careful, a'ight?" I smiled a little and nodded.

"Okay."

After Sean and I parted ways, I walked in my room feeling emotionally exhausted. I sat on the couch and shook my head. Between my confusing feelings for Jesse, talking to Erica, and dealing with Anthony's cold shoulder, I was feeling overwhelmed and anxious. Tears rolled down my face as I sat there.

I felt empty. As happy as I seemed on the outside, I was miserable spiritually. I got up and went inside my room and closed the door and locked it. I sat on my bed and cried. I found myself beginning to do something I hadn't done in a long time: pray. Prayer was once something very important to me, but after Anthony, I couldn't possibly see how I could. After everything I had done, I was sure God was upset with me. I was ashamed. Not only did I have sex with Anthony twice, but I did the same with Jesse. I sighed as words began to fall from my lips:

"God, I'm so sorry. I'm so sorry for neglecting you. I didn't feel like I was worthy enough to come talk to you after everything I had done. I never expected to sleep with anybody, and now I've slept with two people. I've tried to mask my emptiness, but every day is getting harder. I can't go any longer without talking to You. I just want to start over. And I know my virginity is not something I can get back, but I know this guilt and shame is not something I want to experience anymore. Please, forgive me God. I feel so lost without you. I need you. Help me to feel your peace and listen to You. Thank You for still looking out for me even when I stopped talking to You. I truly love You, Lord.

Amen."

I hadn't realized that I ended up on my knees and had my eyes closed. Immediately, I began to feel the emptiness inside fill up. I allowed myself to feel God's presence. I knew He had never left me, but I just ignored the fact that He was there. Peace then came over my body and a smile grew on my face. At that moment, I knew things had to change. The first step was to get closure and have a genuine conversation with Anthony.

Chapter 16

"Do to others as you would have them do to you."
(Luke 6:31)

I woke up the next morning feeling refreshed. I made sure to spend time in God's word and pray because I was determined to get back to my life before Anthony. After I finished my devotion, I decided to text him.

Hey, can we meet up somewhere and talk?

I was hesitant to send the text. He had been giving me the cold shoulder and treated me like he hated me. I took a deep breath and hit send. *He could either say yes or no. If he says yes, cool. If he says, no, that's cool, too. At least I know where we stand, and I'll leave it alone.* Instead of waiting for him to reply, I decided to distract myself. I fixed myself a quick breakfast and picked out my lounging clothes for the day. After about fifteen minutes of distractions, my phone lit up.

Yeah, where you wanna meet?

I sighed in relief as a small smile formed on my face.

On the lawn in an hour.

He texted me back within seconds and said he would be there. While eating my breakfast, it dawned on me that I should tell Jesse. I know we weren't dating, yet, but I wanted to be honest with him. I quickly found his name in my phone and called him. After three rings, he answered.

"Wassup, baby?" he answered.

I smiled, "Hey, Jesse. There's something I want you to know."

He chuckled, "Uh oh."

I laughed, "It's not bad. I'm meeting up with Anthony on the lawn so we can talk. I just don't want there to be any bad blood between us and I need some peace about where we stand."

"Kyrah, you ain't have to tell me that. We not dating, yet."

I sighed, "I know, I know… I just think it's a good way to start off our relationship. Being honest. That's why I wanted to tell you."

He chuckled, "Well, I appreciate it, but I trust you. Go handle your business, a'ight baby?"

I smiled to myself, "Okay. Call me later, Jess."

"I gotchu."

We said goodbye then hung up. I was really happy Jesse was so understanding. I then quickly got up to shower and got ready to meet up with Anthony. It didn't take me long to get dressed, and my hair was still very straight so by the time I finished getting ready completely, it was time to meet him. I headed out of my room and headed downstairs. I got down to the lawn before he did, so I made a little spot with two lawn chairs and waited for him. After waiting for a good five minutes, I finally saw his shadow approaching me. I looked at him. We met eyes. *Stay strong, Kyrah.*

He smiled, "Hey."

I returned a smile, "Hi…"

He sat in the seat that I placed in front of me and looked at me.

"What's up?" he asked.

I sighed, "Anthony… I don't want you to hate me. I don't want there to be any animosity between us."

He shook his head, "I'on hate you Kyrah… I could never hate you. I love you way too much."

"Well, why do you keep treating me like you do? One minute, we're cool and the next minute you have an issue with me."

"Kyrah, what do you expect? The only girl I've ever loved broke up with me and now she wit' somebody else. That's hard for me to see. I ain't wit' that."

I frowned, "Anthony, how do you think I feel? You went right back to Erica literally right after we broke up. Am I wrong?"

He scoffed and leaned back in the chair.

"So, we here to talk about me and Erica? Because what you not gon' do is sit here and trip like all the stuff that went down was my fault."

I looked at him like he had lost his mind. I took a deep breath to calm myself down.

"Anthony, I just want to talk. Can we chill with the attitudes?"

"I don't have an attitude. That's all you."

It took everything in me not to get up and walk away. I knew I couldn't do that because I was the one that invited him to talk. As much as I wanted to just leave him there and move on with my life, I knew we needed this.

"Okay, look, I just want us to be cordial. I don't care about you and Erica and what you guys have going on."

He stared at me and I saw his face soften.

"I can't… I hate that we're not together. I hate knowing that someone else is probably loving you way better than I ever could. I love you, Kyrah. Why can't we try to work it out?"

"Because we just won't work, Anthony. I… I wish things would've gone differently, but they happened how they were supposed to."

He shook his head, "How can you even say that? We had something special. Why you wanna throw that away?"

I thought about what he said. He was right. We did have something special, but it was starting to take a turn for the worse. I felt myself becoming overwhelmed with emotions. All in that moment, I wanted to take Anthony back and work everything out. I knew I couldn't do that, though. Our relationship was too toxic and heavily affected my relationship with God.

"Anthony, you of all people know how I feel about my relationship with God. When I was with you, I wasn't talking to Him as much because I was ashamed of how I felt around you. I wanted you as badly as you wanted me. The struggle to keep my thoughts together was the hardest battle I've ever had to fight. And after we had sex both times, I stopped talking to Him all together because of shame. I'm not blaming anything on you.

I'm blaming everything on myself. We can't be together because I know how I feel around you. I know how badly I want you in every way. I can't go through anymore shame and anymore heartache. And I definitely don't want to stop talking to God anymore. You are a wonderful man, and you were an even better boyfriend. But we won't make it. Not at this point in our lives. I love you, no matter what. You are my first everything. You taught me how to love and how to be loved. And I appreciate you for that. For everything."

He looked at me intensely. A small smile grew on his face.

"You're the only girl I've ever loved. I don't think I could ever love anyone else like I love you. This is hard… I remember when we met. I had to know you. I messed up real bad. I'm sorry, Kyrah. I really am. I ain't mean to push you away. I love you… and I think I always will."

I smiled. I leaned to give him a hug. We stayed like that for about a minute. It was nice to be in his embrace. I would be lying if I said I didn't miss this… Us. Honestly, I wish I could work it out and give us another try. But I knew that would just lead to more sex which would lead to more regret. We parted from one another and looked at each other. I smiled again.

"We good?" I asked.

"Always."

Anthony and I talked for a little while longer before we decided to head back in. I'm glad we were able to find some common ground and squash the hate we were starting to develop for one another. Talking to him made me see the real him that I hadn't seen in a while. I missed him, no doubt, and I was starting to rethink getting into a relationship with Jesse so soon. We weren't dating, yet, and I knew he wasn't rushing the process. But I still feel like he and I were moving pretty fast. Interrupting my thoughts, I heard a knock on my door.

"Come in," I called out. Tamra walked in and made herself comfortable in my lounging chair. I already knew what she was here for. I was dreading telling her about what went down with Jesse.

"We never got to talk about you and Mr. Jesse. What's going on?" she asked.

I nodded. "Well, obviously he and I are very attracted to each other. We took that attraction and had sex on my birthday. We did it twice. At the party and after the party."

She chuckled, "Well, yeah I know that. I heard you guys. I only asked the next day because I was hoping I didn't hear what I thought I heard. And I noticed that you both disappeared at the party so… But are you guys, like, together?"

I shook my head "no" in embarrassment. Our situation was complicated, and I wasn't sure how to explain it.

"No… but we do like each other. He told me that he plans on us getting together, but after my talk with Anthony, I'm not sure I wanna be with anybody else right now. I miss him too much. It's gonna take me a while to get over him."

She nodded, "I understand. You should take some time. I know how much you really love Anthony. And although things didn't work out the way we all thought they would, I know he really loved you, too. He just has some growing up to do. Jesse seems to be a good guy and might be treating you right and giving you the attention you're missing right now, but you need time for you. Why bring another guy into the picture?"

She was right. What was the point? I still had a lot of baggage from Anthony. And after our talk, I was starting to feel some feelings resurface. I was heartbroken. Heartbroken about the fact that we can't be together no matter how much both of us wanted to be.

"When did you realize being with Anthony wasn't good for me?" I asked her after a few moments of silence.

"When you stopped going to your Bible Studies. And it's not like I hated you guys together. It's just… You started changing. I loved you guys together. But I had to tell you that he was changing you. You were becoming more okay with sex. That's not you. And now you've slept with Jesse, too. I'm not judging you in the least bit, but I don't want to see you go down a road that I know you don't want to… And who knows, maybe in the future he'll be different, and you guys can get back together."

I nodded. I was secretly hoping that we could get back together in the future. But the way things were going right now, I just couldn't see that happening. He and I were in two different spaces. And as much as I wanted to be with Jesse, I knew I wasn't ready to be with anybody else. I sighed and hid my face in my hands.

"Don't worry about Jesse. He'll understand. For now, focus on you," Tamra said as she stood up. I removed my hands from my face and looked at her. I nodded in agreement and she walked out of my room.

I sat and pondered on what she said. I shouldn't be worried about Jesse. After all, he did say he would wait for me. But would he really be willing to wait for me considering that I don't even know how long it would take? I sat up and sighed. There was a battle going on in my head on whether I should text Jesse or not. Finally making a decision, I texted him asking him if we could meet up. He quickly texted me back saying he would be at my room in a few minutes. I walked into the living room and sat on the couch and patiently waited for him. Moments later, there was a loud knock on the door. I rolled my eyes as I got up to answer it. As soon I opened the door, he smiled and hugged me, picking me up from the ground.

I laughed, "Jesse, chill."

He laughed with me and placed me back on the ground.

"What's goin' on? You a'ight?" I stared into his light brown eyes and smiled. *Maybe I'm trippin'.*

I nodded, "Yeah, I'm fine. I just wanted to see you."

He smiled his gorgeous smile, "Aw, how sweet. Let me in so I can kiss you."

I laughed and moved out of his way so he could come in. He leaned down and slowly kissed me on the lips. He made himself comfortable on the couch and I followed him. As I was going to sit beside him, he grabbed my waist and pulled me on his lap.

"I thought you weren't gonna kiss me until we got together," I joked.

He smirked and stared at me, "I couldn't help myself. Why you text me for real?"

While I was trying to come up with a lie, he laughed.

"Don't lie, either. You a bad liar, anyway." I rolled my eyes and laughed.

"I just… I was thinking that maybe I wasn't ready to be with you, but then I saw you at the door and how happy you were to see me… I see that you wanna be with me. But I don't know how long it's gonna take me to get over my breakup, and I don't wanna keep you waiting."

We sat in silence for a few seconds which really made me nervous. Fear rose in my chest because I know indication of what he was going to say or how he was going to react. I took a deep breath as I waited for him to respond.

"I mean, it ain't like you asked me to wait for you. I like you, for real, Kyrah. When you really care for someone, you don't care how long it takes because you see the end picture. I see us together. I see you happy. Hell, I can see us married with whole buncha' kids, if that's what you want."

I giggled, "I like you, a lot. I really hope we can be together and be happy."

He smiled and bit his bottom lip, slightly. "We will, baby girl. I promise to give you the world. I told you I wasn't going anywhere. I keep my word, shawty." He winked and made me giggle. I stared at his lips hoping he would get the hint.

"Gon' head and kiss me since you dyin' to." I smiled and leaned in to kiss him. It was something so innocent about his kisses that I loved. All the doubts that I was beginning to have started to fade away. I heard what everyone was telling me and warning me about, but maybe Jesse was different. I no longer cared about what everyone else thought. I liked him and I wanted us to be together.

"A'ight, now. Chill. I really wanna help you stick to your morals, but you can't be teasin' me," he said as he broke the almost heated kiss.

I laughed, "I'm sorry. I really appreciate that, Jesse. You're so sweet. You're everything. I'm glad we're going to give this a shot."

"I'm glad you're giving me a shot." He smiled and kissed me on my forehead. *This could be a good thing...*

Chapter 17

"For I am convinced that neither death nor life, neither angels nor demons, neither the present nor the future, nor the powers, neither height nor depth, nor anything else in all creation , will be able to separate us from the love of God that is in Christ Jesus our Lord." (Romans 8:38-39)

"Alright, everyone, we only have a few weeks left together. Make sure you stay on top of your game! I'll see you all next week. Have a great weekend!" my English professor stated ending our class. I packed my things and walked out of the classroom. It's been a few weeks since my talk with Anthony and everything had been smoothly. Jesse and I were still in the "talking" stage and I appreciated how he was willing to take things slow with me. But I hadn't seen him all week and it was sort of bothering me.

Jesse's a pretty busy person, so I tried not to think too much into it. Trying to ignore my paranoid thoughts, I proceeded to walk down the hallway. As I was about to put my earphones in my ears, I felt someone grab my waist from behind. I almost panicked until I heard the person's voice.

“Hey, boo,” the voice said in my ear. I rolled my eyes and turned around to find Jesse. I crossed my arms and frowned.

He pouted, “You ain’t happy to see me?”

I bit my lip trying to hide my smile. “Yeah, I’m happy to see you, but you almost gave me a heart attack! What’s wrong with you?” I hit him on his right arm, and he laughed.

“Dang, my bad. I aint’ mean to scare you.” He moved closer and grabbed my waist. He pulled me closer to him with my arms still crossed. “Stop acting stubborn and give me a kiss.”

I smirked and just stared at him. He smacked his teeth and leaned in to kiss me against my will. It didn’t take long for me to give in and kiss him back.

We parted and he chuckled. “You couldn’t resist me, even if you wanted to.”

I rolled my eyes, “Whatever.”

He smiled and stared at me. I blushed becoming intimidated by his stares.

“I know it’s last minute and pretty impromptu, but I’m off tonight. I wanna take you out on a date. Officially. Plus, I know you ain’t doin’ nothin’ anyway.”

I laughed at his last statement. “Oh, shut up!”

He laughed with me, “No, seriously. Whatchu say? I wanna take you out, for real.”

I smiled and nodded, “Okay. Sounds good.”

He smiled, “A’ight. I’ll text you the details. I gotta go to class. I’ll see you later. Text me when you get to your room.” He kissed me on the forehead then the lips.

“Okay,” I responded with a smile. We parted and headed our opposite ways.

Two hours passed and Jesse texted me telling me that he would be up to get me at 8. It was now 6:45. I beginning to feel anxiety about this date. It felt like my first date with Anthony all over again. I was starting to feel the exact same way I felt that night and I was legitimately afraid of how far things may go after this date tonight. I wanted to be with Jesse, but everything was holding me back.

After losing the battle in my head, I decided to start getting ready. I took a shower and brushed my teeth. After doing my hygiene routine, I picked out an outfit. He hadn’t told me how to dress, but I was just going to wing it. I knew if I asked him, he would just start a play argument with me, and I was too nervous to entertain his silliness right now. I settled on a peach colored crop top, some black high waist jeans that hugged my hips, a long black cardigan, and some black wedges that had an ankle strap. I put on some pearl stud earrings and wore my natural hair in a big puff. I remembered Jesse telling me how he likes when I wear it like that.

I rolled my cardigan sleeves up slightly and put some light makeup on with a nude lip. Once I finished getting ready, I checked the time. *7:50. Perfect timing.* Jesse then texted me asking me if I was ready and I quickly responded that I was. I grabbed the purse that I wanted to carry, my phone, and my room keys and walked out of my room. After I locked my door, I went into the living room area and waited for Jesse. Tamra and Raynah walked in the front door and looked at me in confusion.

"You goin' out without us, girl?" Tamra joked.

I smiled, "No, Jesse's taking me on a date. It was kind of a last-minute thing."

Raynah smiled widely. "I told you the night of your party you were gonna snatch another dude up. I knew it. You looked too fine that night not to. You look fine tonight, too, girl!"

We all laughed. Right as I was going to answer her, there was a loud obnoxious knock on our door.

"Ay, open the door! I hear, y'all!" Jesse yelled from the other side. I rolled my eyes and stood from the seat I was sitting in. Tamra opened the door and frowned.

"Why are you so annoying?" she asked him.

He chuckled, "Hello to you, too. Where my baby at?"

I walked to the door so he could see me. He bit his lip and smirked.

"Hey, beautiful."

"Hey, shawty." He laughed and grabbed my hand pulling me closer to him. Since he was much taller than me, my face was at his chest with these heels on. He leaned down and kissed me softly. "Ready?" he asked. I nodded and smiled.

"Have fun, you two cuties. Have her back in one piece, Jesse," Tamra stated.

"You see her, right? I'll try," he replied honestly. We all laughed, and Jesse and I left the room. We joked all the way downstairs. I loved being around him because I really felt like I could be myself. As we were walking out of our building, we walked past Anthony and some of his friends. I wasn't anticipating seeing him at all because I wasn't sure what mood he was in today. I sort of held my breath as we approached him. He looked up and saw us. He had a pained expression on his face but played it off by giving a small smile. He nodded his head at both of us and I waved. Jesse saluted him and we proceeded to walk past him. *That went better than I thought it would.*

“So, you like the restaurant?” Jesse asked as we sat at our table waiting for our waiter. We were at a cute little spot downtown that was very intimate. I loved it because I just knew the food would be great.

I smiled and nodded. “It’s cute… And quaint.” I looked around then back at Jesse. He smirked and nodded. Our waitress soon came to our table with a warm smile.

“I see I have two little love birds,” she laughed. “My name’s Jamie and I’ll be taking care you two cuties tonight. What can I get you to drink?”

I smiled amused at her enthusiasm. She was a very pretty lady that looked like she was in her early forties. She looked at me and waited for me to tell her what I wanted to drink. I opened my mouth to speak but Jesse stopped me.

“Wait, bae, lemme order for you. I wanna see if I remember what you like,” he said concentrating on the drink section of the menu.

I laughed, “Have at it.”

"She will have… Hm… A lemonade… Right?" I nodded and smiled. He winked and chuckled, "And I'll have a sweet tea."

Jamie smiled widely, "Alright. I'll be right back with y'all's drinks." She walked away and I giggled.

"Whatcha laughin' at?" Jesse asked looking up at me.

"You. You really pay attention."

"Of course. That's my job. Gotta keep my baby happy." He smiled his gorgeous smile. I blushed. We talked a little bit more and our waitress came back with our drinks a little while later. She took our food orders and left us alone again. The rest of dinner went so naturally. We talked and whenever it was silent, it wasn't awkward. It was assurance that I was making the right decision.

On the way back to the school, we decided to stop and get some ice cream. We sat at the nearby park, in the late-night breeze. He looked at me and smiled.

"You really look beautiful. You always look beautiful, but I feel special that you got all dolled up for me."

I chuckled, "Yeah, don't get used to it. When we start dating, I will get comfortable."

He laughed, "You'll still be beautiful to me. I've seen you in a lot of ways, if you know what I mean." I burst into a hard laughter. He joined me and we both calmed down a little. "But you're always beautiful to me. I'on know… Something about you is so special. Like, I've never been the type to wanna settle down, feel me? But you make me want to." I listened to him intently as we both stared off into space. I paid close attention to every word he was saying.

He looked at me and I looked at him. "I'm ready if you ready. Will you be my girlfriend, Kyrah?"

I smiled and nodded, "I would love to, Jesse." He smiled and leaned in to kiss me. That moment was perfect. I swear fireworks could have gone off if they wanted to. It was so magical. At that moment, I knew that this was the right thing.

The ride back to the school was perfect. It seemed like Jesse and I were moving at a perfect pace. I was excited to see where this relationship would go. Saying "yes" just naturally floated from my lips and I didn't regret it at all. After we arrived back to the school, we took our time getting back to my room. Once we got there, we realized we were alone. In the back of my mind, I thought about asking him to leave or us going somewhere where there were other people around, but we just sat on the couch and talked like we hadn't just spent the evening together.

“Do you feel comfortable with me being here and no one else here? I can leave,” he randomly offered.

I smiled, “I was hesitant about it at first, but it’s cool. You don’t have to leave, yet.” He stared at me and bit his bottom lip. He scanned my body making me blush.

“Actually, I do…” We laughed as he stood up. “I gotta get outta here before I take you to your room and give you a repeat of your birthday. I’ve been struggling all night trying not to go there.”

I chuckled, “Well, then, goodbye.”

He frowned, “Damn, okay. Where’s my kiss?” I stood up and moved closer to him. We stared at each other for a while. He raised one eyebrow and bit his bottom lip as he pulled me towards him. I smiled while blushing. He leaned down and kissed me sweetly. We kissed for what felt like eternity. We parted and just stayed in each other’s arms. I rested my head on his chest and listened to his heartbeat. He rested his chin on top of my head and kissed it.

“Don’t feel bad about wanting me, Jesse. I want you, too. But I appreciate you respecting me.” I looked up at him and he smiled. He kissed my forehead and we parted.

“I respect you because you respect yourself. I’ll come see you tomorrow. Goodnight, baby.” He kissed me once more before walking towards the door.

"Goodnight, love." I smiled as I watched him leave. I sat back on the couch and just thought about everything that happened tonight. Everything was so perfect. Although Jesse said our date was impromptu and last minute, he made it feel as if he had really taken him time to plan it. It was so simple, but it was everything. And now that we were officially dating, I couldn't wait to take on this new journey with him.

Tamra and Raynah walked in interrupting my thoughts not too long after. They looked at me and smiled.

"You got clothes on! So, y'all ain't have sex or anything, right?" Raynah asked.

I laughed, "The opportunity presented itself, but he said he had to leave because he didn't want that to happen. He has this thing about keeping me a good girl, so he doesn't want us to sleep together anymore."

Tamra came and sat beside me while smiling a little. "That's really sweet. So, are y'all exclusive now?" I nodded and blushed.

"Yeah." Tamra studied my face and a concerned expression spread across her face.

"Kyrah, are you sure you're ready to be with someone else?" Without hesitation I nodded.

"Absolutely." She smiled and nodded, leaving it alone.

“Well,” Raynah began, “I don’t wanna hype anything up like I did with Anthony, but Jesse has you glowing… You sure y’all ain’t have sex?”

I rolled my eyes and laughed, “I promise. I’m just happy.”

Chapter 18

"In him we have redemption through his blood, the forgiveness of sins, in accordance with the riches of God's grace" (Ephesians 1:7)

I woke up the next day around 7:00 in the morning feeling completely sick. Trying to figure out why I was up so early, I slowly sat up because I knew if I moved anymore, I was going to puke. I sighed.

"Uh oh…" I said quietly before getting up and running to the bathroom. I puked like I never had before. Once I finished, I sat by the toilet feeling slightly weak. A soft knock on the door startled me.

"Come in," I responded in a weak voice. Tamra slowly opened the door and peeped her head in.

"You okay, girl?" she asked concern as she knelt beside me.

I shrugged, "I don't know. I might have food poisoning or something. I just woke up feeling extremely tired. I just wanna go back to sleep."

She nodded, "Yeah, go lay back down. If you need me, text me." I nodded and gave her a small smile. She smiled back and left me alone in the bathroom. I rubbed my head and sighed. I finally stood up, flushed the toilet and went back in my room. I lied back in my bed and stared at the ceiling. The nausea feeling was still there, but I was fine. I decided to text Jesse to see if he was okay. He had to work at 8 so I knew he was awake.

Hey, I just got really sick and just threw up. Are you ok? I want to make sure it's not the food from last night.

I placed my phone beside me and waited for him to text me back. After almost drifting off to sleep, my phone vibrated continuously. I rolled my eyes when I saw that he was calling me. *Only he would call instead of texting back.*

"Hello?" I answered, my voice still very weak.

"Baby, you a'ight?" he asked in an alarmed voice.

I chuckled, "I'm fine. I think it's just something I ate last night."

"Okay. I was just making sure. I'ma come see you when I get off work, a'ight? Just rest and chill today. Take it easy. I'll come take care of you later."

"Yes sir."

He laughed, "A'ight, I gotta go. I'll call back during my break. Bye, baby."

"Bye, sweetie." I hung up the phone and tried going back to sleep. After about thirty minutes, I began drifting back into a deep sleep…

"Kyrah," I heard faintly from outside the door. I slowly opened my eyes and frowned. *What time is it?* "Kyrah, boo," I heard the voice again.

"Come in," I finally said, my voice still a little weak. *Why do I still sound like that?* The door opened and in walked Tamra.

"Hey, how you feelin'?" she asked as she sat on the foot of my bed.

I shrugged, "I'm okay. Still feel a little sick. I'm tired, too. I feel a little weak."

She nodded and looked away as if she was in deep thought about something. She looked back at me with concern.

"Kyrah, I don't think you have food poisoning."

I chuckled, "Why?"

"When was the last time you had your period?"

I shrugged, "I don't know… It's supposed to come on…" I drifted as my eyes got big. "It was supposed to come on last week… Tamra! Oh my gosh! This can't be happening…"

She scooted closer as she saw tears forming in my eyes. "It's okay, girl. We won't know until you take a test. We can go buy some. You need to know."

I shook my head and hid my face in my hands. I began to sob. *This can't be happening...*

"Well? Are you pregnant?" Tamra asked as we waited for the third pregnancy test to tell us if it was positive or not. Raynah waited anxiously with a sad look on her face. I hesitantly looked at the test.

"It's negative, guys. They're all negative. I'm not pregnant." I sighed in relief and silently thanked God. They exhaled slowly as their faces became softer.

"That was close," Raynah said lowly. I nodded agreeing with her. I suddenly thought about Jesse. Although I wasn't pregnant, I needed to tell him about my scare.

We all sat in silence until Tamra broke it. "Are you going to tell Jesse?" she asked.

I nodded my head. I had to tell him what was going on. Since he was planning on coming by later, it would be wise to go ahead and tell him. I didn't exactly want to, but I knew he would want to know. I guess I was just nervous about how he would react.

For the rest of the day I just stayed in my room thinking. I needed to stop thinking so much. *I can't believe I almost got pregnant. Didn't we use protection? I guess they don't always guarantee you won't get knocked up. Oh, God. Thanks for having my back. I'm not ready to be a mom. That's just too much responsibility. Lord, I don't know what-* My thoughts were interrupted by my phone ringing repeatedly. I looked at my phone and saw "My Lil' Shawty" with heart emojis appear on the screen. I quickly answered the phone.

"Hey, prince," I answered.

"Prince? That's new… I like it."

I laughed, "I figured you would. What's up?"

He chuckled, "I said I'd call you. How are you feeling, baby?"

I sighed. I was hesitant to tell him. I thought it would be better to talk in person. "I'm fine. Just… wasn't feeling well."

"Well, what was wrong? Don't lie either."

I smiled, "I won't. We'll talk later. I'd rather us do it in person."

"Oh, a'ight. We'll talk in a few hours. I might actually be able to get off early so I'ma come through soon, a'ight bae?"

"Okay. I'll see you later, boo-boo."

He laughed, "These nicknames. Bye, baby." I giggled and hit the "End" option on my phone.

I spent the next few hours preparing for Jesse to come. I decided to take another shower and put on some cuter lounging clothes. I figured I should at least be decent looking for my boyfriend. After waiting and straightening up for about three hours, there was an obnoxious knock on the door. I rolled my eyes already knowing it was Jesse being extra.

"Ay, open the door! I hear you moving around, Kyrah!" he yelled from the other side. I swung the door open and stared at him with one hand on my hip.

"Why you gotta be so extra with life?" I asked pretending to be annoyed.

He laughed grabbing my waist and pulling me closer to him. I looked up him trying to keep a straight face but failing completely. I smiled as I stared into his eyes. He moved closer and leaned down to kiss me. He kissed me like he hadn't seen me all week. Once we parted, I looked down and blushed. He pecked me on my forehead and moved past me to get inside our room. I followed him and we both sat on the couch.

"So, wassup witcha? You straight?" he asked as he patted me on the leg.

I shrugged, "Well, you should know… That I took a few pregnancy tests…"

He eyes got big as he stared at me. He didn't respond for a while, which scared me. A minute passed and he still didn't say anything. Becoming annoyed, I rolled my eyes.

"Jesse!" I exclaimed removing him from his thoughts.

He looked at me with blank face, "H-huh?"

"Are you okay?"

He nodded. "I'm cool. I was just thinkin'… I thought we used protection… How? —"

I chuckled, "I'm not pregnant, babe. Calm down. We did. Maybe one of the condoms had a hole in it. It was just a scare. I'm a week late and the sickness just got to me."

He sighed in relief, "Oh, good. I mean… I ain't ready for all'at. And I know you not either. We should be more careful."

I nodded, "I'm definitely not. No kids until I get married."

He laughed, "Yeah, definitely."

It was quite for a moment. Both of us were too lost in our own "what ifs" and "how's" to say anything. The possibility of me being pregnant scared me to the core. I couldn't even imagine the scenario of having to tell my parents about it. A rush of thankfulness and relief flooded my body as I thought about the many bullets we'd just dodged. I touched his arm and he looked at me.

"You okay?" I asked sincerely.

He smiled, "Yeah, I'm good, baby." He leaned in and kissed me lightly on the lips. His fondness of me was so obvious and I'm glad he wasn't afraid to show it.

We chilled on the couch for the next couple of hours just talking and laughing. There was a never a dull moment with him. I hadn't even realized that we hadn't turned on the television nor had either of us checked our phones. At about 10 that night, Jesse decided that it was time for him to leave, and I can't even deny my disappointment.

I gave him sad eyes and poked out my bottom lip. He chuckled, "Don't do that, boo. You'll force me to stay."

I kept the face, "But that's the point, Jesse."

He laughed and moved closer to me. Our faces were inches apart, making me lose my breath.

"I gotta go because nothing good happens after 10:00 and you know that. We'll hang out all day tomorrow. I'm off. We'll do whatever you want, a'ight?" He pecked me on the lips repeatedly making me laugh.

"Okay, okay!" We laughed as we parted. I walked him to the door, and he turned around to kiss me one more time.

"I'll see you tomorrow, baby." He kissed me slowly and I bit my bottom lip.

"Okay, Prince." He smirked and walked out of the door. I happily watched him walk down the hallway until he disappeared around the corner. I closed the door and made my way into my room. I debated on if I wanted to wait up for Tamra and Raynah, but quickly decided against it once I realized how sleepy I was.

After changing into some comfortable pajamas, I lied on my bed and browsed my Instagram. A smile appeared on my face when I saw the picture Jesse took of me. I read the caption "Isn't she beautiful?" and blushed. I spent a few more minutes scrolling on my news feed until I decided to put my phone down for the night. I closed my eyes and began to say a silent prayer.

God, thank you for having my back. That was a close call. Babies are beautiful, and I want to be a mom one day... But today is not that day. I smiled to myself and eventually dozed off into a deep sleep.

Chapter 19

"I love you, Lord, my strength." (Psalm 18:1)

"I'm gonna miss you guys so much. I can't believe this school year is over already. What am I gonna do without y'all?" Tamra said in a sad voice as we were all packing our things. It's officially the last day before we have to move out of our dorms and go home. I gave her a sad smile and sighed.

"Yeah, I'm gonna miss you guys, too," I responded looking down.

Raynah laughed, "Yeah, you're gonna miss us, but you lookin' down because you're gonna miss Jesse the most. Don't play." We laughed because it was true. I already missed Jesse and we hadn't left yet. Suddenly, there was a loud obnoxious knock on our door and we already knew who it was.

"Speaking of the devil," Tamra said loudly rolling her eyes.

"Ay! I ain't no devil! Open the door and don't keep me waiting! Baby, tell them to open the door!" he yelled.

I laughed and went to open the door. I stood there and stared at him with a frown. He frowned back.

"What?" he asked puzzled.

"Why do you do that every time you come over here? You don't have to be so extra."

He smiled and walked towards me as he pulled me close to him. "You gon' miss it. Don't even try to deny it, either." He leaned down and kissed my forehead then my nose. He stared at me in my eyes and smiled.

I bit my bottom lip, "I am gonna miss it… And you."

He nodded, "Me too." He looked away with a sad look on his face.

"Hey", I frowned, "What's wrong?"

He grabbed my hand and led me to my room and closed the door. He sighed and at sat on my bed.

"Baby, what is going on?" I asked as I sat beside him.

He took a deep breath before looking at me. "I… It's been a few weeks since you had that pregnancy scare, but I can't help but think about it every time I see you. I just keep thinking about how we almost had a kid together. We're too young for all that, but I just want you to know that I would've supported you in any way I could… Anyway, I guess I said all of that to say that I'm really feelin' you. This whole scare just made me realize how much I care about you as a person and as my girlfriend. We haven't been together that long, but you do mean a lot to me, Kyrah."

I smiled and my eyes got big. I leaned in and kissed him passionately. I quickly stopped myself before it got too carried away. It seemed like we were moving at this fast pace, but I couldn't deny the love that growing in my heart for him.

Staring in his eyes, I smiled. "I really appreciate that, Jesse." He smirked and leaned in to kiss me again. Suddenly the door swung open and Tamra and Raynah burst in. We looked at them with puzzled and slightly annoyed facial expressions.

"What? Don't look at us like that. We're just makin' sure y'all not in here being nasty," Tamra stated with her hands on her hips.

"Nah, I would've locked the door and you definitely would've heard her," Jesse responded. I hit him on his arm making him laugh.

"Y'all wanna go get something to eat? I'm hungry and it's our last time," Raynah suggested. We all agreed and made our way out of my room. After all of us locked our doors, we headed downstairs and out of the building. I couldn't deny the fact that I was feeling extremely sad that we were all about to leave each other for the summer. Although we would eventually come back together, it was still sad. On the ride to the restaurant, Jesse and I held hands the whole time. We arrived at an Applebee's not too far from the school shortly and made our way inside. We were seated in a secluded booth as soon as we walked in. After our waiter came and we took our drink and appetizer orders, it became unusually quiet.

"Why y'all so quiet? I don't like it," Jesse said breaking the silence.

Raynah chuckled, "This is pretty sad. What am I gonna do without you guys?"

I smiled and looked down at my lap. We had been through so much together this year. Even Jesse and I had been through quite a bit in our short time knowing each other.

"I have to say, Jesse, you have quite a strong girlfriend," Tamra said looking back and forth between both of us. I looked up from my lap and looked at Tamra curiously. "Girl, you have been through a lot for your freshman year. You started out as a shy, quiet person, but then you met Anthony. And although I hate what you guys had to go through and how it affected you, I'm glad he broke you out of your shell. You went to your first party and got drunk, you made new friends, you met Jesse, and you're back on track with your relationship with God," she paused, "You've grown as a person. I'll admit, I was concerned after you slept with Jesse because I thought you were becoming a sex addict." We all laughed at the last part.

“But it’s good to see you make a turn around and really grow as a young woman.” My heart warmed at her words causing me to smile.

“Thanks, Tam. I think this year has been a learning experience for me.” She smiled and nodded in agreement.

Moments later, our waiter was back with our drinks and soon our appetizers arrived. The rest of our meal was filled with laughs and conversation about our summer plans. We had even decided that we would pick one week out of the summer to take a trip with the whole crew. After we all finished eating, we headed back to the school to finish packing the last of our things. Jesse walked us to our room but kept me behind in the hallway with him. After Tamra and Raynah left us alone in the hallway and I looked at Jesse with a confused expression.

He gently backed me into the wall and kissed me. I smiled in the kiss. I was going to miss this so much. I was going to miss everything about Jesse. Of course, he could easily drive down to see me, but it would be different not seeing him every day. This kiss reminded me of how we first met and how we instantly clicked. I almost wondered how different things would be if we had met sooner. Would I have even dated Anthony? Although I did still miss Anthony a little, I felt that I was finally over him. I really like Jesse. And despite the fact that we slept together before we started dating and all the warnings everyone gave me about getting involved with him, I love that he still made the effort to be with me.

We parted and stared at each other. Random tears escaped my eyes and I looked down. I hadn't realized how sad I was about us not being together every day this summer. Jesse grabbed my face, gently, and wiped my tears away.

"Don't cry, baby girl." He chuckled sadly making me a laugh a bit. I looked up at him, which only made me cry more.

"I can't help it. I'm gonna miss you."

He smiled, "I'ma miss you, too, boo. We'll see each other this summer, though. Don't worry. Stop cryin'. I'm not dyin'." I laughed and rolled my eyes. I wiped the rest of the tears that had fallen.

"I know, I know. Don't judge me. Just let me cry it out. At least now I know I won't cry tomorrow. I'll be ready to get rid of you by then."

"Please," he scoffed, "You couldn't get rid of me. You love me too much, anyway."

I smiled, "I do."

Chapter 20

"We were therefore buried with him through baptism into death in order that, just as Christ was raised from the dead through the glory of the Father, we too may live a new life. (Romans 6:4)"

I checked around my room to make sure I got everything. It was sad to see how empty my room was, but I was somewhat happy to be going home.

"You got everything?" my dad asked as he walked in.

"Yeah. Everything is empty." He smiled and nodded. He walked out of my room leaving me alone. I sighed and looked around. So many memories in this room. So many tears. So many laughs. So many arguments and confessions. Everything I experienced this year came rushing back to me. I smiled as I thought about all of the good memories. Anthony suddenly popped in my head and I wondered if he was still on campus. After debating on whether or not to go see him, I finally gave in.

"I'll be right back. I'm going to say bye to one of my friends," I told my parents before I walked out.

"Okay, don't be too long. We need to hit the road," my dad replied. I playfully rolled my eyes in my head at him rushing me. I nodded and continued out of the door. I began feeling weird and nervous and started regretting going to his room. I reached his floor and found his room. I took a deep breath before knocking on the door. I anxiously waited for him to come to the door and suddenly the door swung open. He looked at me surprised and smiled.

“Hey, wassup?” he greeted.

I smiled back, “Hey. I didn’t know if you had left, yet. I just wanted to come say bye. I’m about to leave.”

He chuckled, “You could’ve just texted me.”

I rolled my eyes, “Anthony, don’t start—”

He held his hands up like he was surrendering and laughed. “I was joking. Chill.” I laughed with him. We stood in silence for a moment.

“Do you wanna come in?” he asked.

I shook my head, “I have to get going. My dad is already rushing me,” I rolled my eyes. “But I just wanted to come say goodbye to my friend.”

He smiled and held his arms out, “I appreciate it, really.” I chuckled and hugged him. We stayed like that for a while until I finally removed myself from his embrace.

“I’m gonna miss you,” he admitted.

I nodded suddenly becoming sad. “Yeah, me too. But we’ll see each other next year.”

He nodded, “Always thinking positively.”

I laughed, “I have to. That’s just me.”

He smirked and looked down.

“I should get going, but you enjoy your summer, Anthony.” I smiled and he looked at me returning it.

“You too, Kyrah.” I smiled one last time before walking away. I was glad Anthony and I were finally in a place where we could be cordial with one another. At times, I still wondered what could’ve been between us, but all in all, I knew it was time to truly let it go. As I finally made my way back to my room, I found Tamra and Raynah both sitting on the couch.

“You guys still here?” I asked shocked.

Tamra nodded, “We just wanted to sit here for a minute before we left. Your parents are downstairs, and they said come out when you’re ready.” I nodded and joined them on the couch.

“I’m really going to miss you guys. This school year was way better than I expected it to be,” Raynah stated with a sad expression.

“Yeah, me too. I miss you guys already,” Tamra responded looking at both of us.

I chuckled, “You guys, we’ll be back in two months. And we’re planning that trip this summer. That should be fun.”

Tamra rolled her eyes, “You always gotta be so positive. Let me be sad.” I laughed thinking how Anthony just told me the same thing. I smacked my teeth.

“I know, I know. I can’t help it.”

She smiled, “I’m definitely gonna miss it, though. But you’re right. We’ll see each other sometime this summer.” Raynah and I nodded in agreement. My phone randomly vibrated in my hand and I checked it to see a text from my mom. **We’re ready. Come on.** I sighed as I stood up.

“I gotta go,” I stated sadly. They stood up with me and attacked me in a hug. I laughed hugging them back.

“Come walk me downstairs” I suggested. They agreed and we all headed downstairs. As we walked towards the parking lot, I saw my parents in their truck and I walked to my car, which was parked behind them. The plan was to trail behind them on the way home. I opened the driver’s side and turned to look at my roommates. I poked out my bottom lip and they laughed.

"See you guys soon. I miss you guys," I said holding out my arms for a group hug. They made dramatic crying noises and hugged me.

"I miss you, too, baby!" Tamra exclaimed.

"Me too!" Raynah replied. I laughed as we all separated. I got in my car and they backed away as I closed my door. My dad started the truck and began to drive off. I started my car and looked at them one last time. I waved and followed my dad. I almost couldn't believe I had successfully completed my first year of college. There were many things that I was going to miss and many things I wasn't. The most important thing I learned was definitely how much God cared about me. Through everything I experienced while being here, God was always there. Even when I decided to do my own thing and I felt I let Him down, He was still there through it all.

I barely acknowledged Him during that time, but I was thankful and in love with the fact that He was still waiting for me to talk to Him about what I was dealing with. I'm thankful for Him bringing Anthony into my life and showing me that I can truly love someone, sometimes the timing is just off. I'm also thankful for Anthony showing me how to forgive and let things go, all while keeping it real. I'm thankful for God showing me how to be the bigger person when it came to dealing with Erica. As much as I wanted to be rude and basically fight her, I'm glad He showed me that having grace on others will get me a lot further than fighting evil with evil.

And last but certainly not least, I'm super thankful for Jesse. Our relationship started on an unusual note and that made me hesitant initially. But even though we slept together before we even acknowledged the feelings we had for one another, I was still thankful that we were able to build something from it. Being with him taught me how to let stuff go and move on. He taught me how to forgive myself. Everything I went through this school year really changed my life for the better.

My phone then randomly vibrated repeatedly, and I frowned. I checked it really quick to see Jesse calling me. I smiled and answered.

"Yes, Jesse?"

He laughed, "I miss you, baby. Come back!!" I laughed at his over-exaggeration.

"Aren't you coming to see me this weekend?"

"Just let me miss you, girl."

I laughed, "My bad. I miss you, too."

"You better. But yeah, I'm definitely coming to see you this weekend. I took this weekend off to come down to spend time with you."

I sighed, "Darn… Just when I thought I got rid of you." He chuckled then smacked his teeth.

"A'ight, you know what? Let me get off this phone before I cuss you out."

I laughed, "I was kidding! I can't wait to see you. For real. I miss you, baby."

He laughed, "I know. But I'ma let you go. I know you drivin' so you need to pay attention since you'on have no sense of direction anyway."

I smacked my teeth, "Whatever, bye. I'll call you later."

He laughed, "You better." He ended the call, and I placed my phone in my lap. I smiled to myself and enjoyed the rest of the ride home. *What a year…*

To Be Continued...

About Author

Karmen Scott, a wife and mother of two, is an Augusta, Georgia native. She received her high school diploma from Lucy Craft Laney High School in 2014 and her bachelor's degree in marketing from Brenau University in 2020. She is currently working towards her master's in clinical mental health counseling from Walden University. However, Karmen's first love is writing.

Karmen attended Georgia Gwinnett College from 2014-2017 where she wrote her very first novel, Inexperienced her freshman year. Although she wears many hats, writing will always be her passion. She is the founder of Child of Purpose, LLC and has a blog where she writes inspirational pieces to encourage her followers. Karmen hopes to continue her journey as a writer and published author in the years to come.

To learn more and follow her journey, visit www.childofpurposeblog.wordpress.com.

Purchase the sequel of the Inexperienced Series: Over-Experienced

Milton Keynes UK
Ingram Content Group UK Ltd.
UKHW020921120224
437701UK00013B/520

9 798869 097538